As Within So Without

As Within So Without

& other writings

Daniel Barbiero

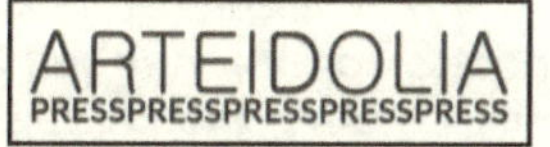

New York

As Within So Without

ARTEIDOLIA PRESS
P.O. Box 157
New York, N.Y. 10276

Book design · ARTEIDOLIA PRESS
Cover photograph · Randee Silv

arteidolia.com/arteidolia-press

First Edition
Library of Congress Control Number: 2021913295
ISBN: 978-1-7369983-0-4

The eye's plain version is a thing apart,
The vulgate of experience.

Wallace Stevens, *An Ordinary Evening in New Haven*

Abandonnées les rênes du sens commun, une
autre espèce de sense pressant, divinatoire, guide
l'homme vers où il veut aller sans le savoir.

André Breton, *Le Merveilleux contre le mystère*

φύσις κρύπτεσθαι φιλεῖ

Heraclitus, DK B123

Acknowledgements

The twenty essays collected here contain ideas that have been crystallizing since the late 1970s but only relatively recently have been given the form they seem to have wanted to take from the beginning (if only I'd known then). All twenty were published in Arteidolia, an online journal of the arts I first discovered in 2014. I don't recall now exactly what brought me there, but I do remember reading a long review by patrick brennan and being impressed with the kind of intellectual depth and personal expression the journal clearly seemed to encourage. My own experiences in writing for Arteidolia since then have only served to reinforce that initial impression.

Over the years the journal and editor Randee Silv has indulged me in allowing me to write about whatever interests me, in whatever form I thought appropriate. Silv's editing style has been a happy combination of light-handedness and astute suggestion, and to her goes my deep gratitude for her unstinting encouragement and truly collaborative attitude toward editing. This book literally would not have come to be without her suggestion that I do it. patrick brennan has also provided invaluable input and stimulating discussion, particularly on the topic of improvisation, which has been a lifetime's work for both of us.

Creative inspiration has come from a good number of artists and others I've had the pleasure of working with or conversing with—far too many to name exhaustively, but chief among them Ken Manheimer; Nancy Havlik, whose Dance Performance Group had me as musical director for several years; my long-time ensemble Colla

Parte (Perry Conticchio, Rich O'Meara and the late Kevin O'Meara); my friend and regular collaborator Cristiano Bocci, whose suggestion of the concept of non-places for our second album led to one of the essays included here; and Ettore Garzia, whose friendship and support have always been warmly appreciated. No acknowledgment would be complete without mention of my comrades and co-conspirators in the DC area experimental music scene—Gary Rouzer, Jeff Surak, Chris Videll, and a host of others who over the years have been a reliable source of friendship, provocative sounds and good cheer, in roughly equal amounts.Special thanks to Janice Goldblum, who proof-read these pieces at one time or another, and to Val Deale, whose loaning me his copy of Chipp's Theories of Modern Art back in the summer of 1979 got this whole thing started, though he doesn't know it.

And finally, I'd like to acknowledge my wife and son, who throughout this project have cheerfully put up with a husband and father even more distracted than usual.

• • •

Is Silence Golden? is an expanded version of an essay that originally appeared in the June, 2018 issue of Perfect Sound Forever, and is reproduced here with the kind permission of PSF and editor Jason Gross.

Parts of *Joëlle Léandre: Being with Sound* originally appeared as a review published in Avant Music News in October, 2011 and are included here with thanks to AMN and editor Mike Borella.

Atopia: Soundings From Non-places" began life as the liner note to Non-places, an album of composed and improvised music created in collaboration with Cristiano Bocci.

All of the essays in *As Within So Without: & other writings* were published on Arteidolia between 2015 and 2021.

CONTENTS

Introduction

As Within, So Without: the title of this collection of essays, written over the past ten years, is a parodistic paraphrase of the old hermetic formula often translated as "As Above, So Below." The phrase has been interpreted as describing, in condensed form, a purported system of correspondences binding together the greater cosmos and the smaller human world.

The title of the present collection, like the phrase it parodies, also expresses the idea of a mutual implication of worlds—in this case what could be called, for lack of a better metaphor, the interior world of the individual person, and the exterior world in which that person is situated. It is a mutual implication based on a relationship of permeability and reciprocal formation that in turn is expressed as a network of meanings, both personal and impersonal, that disclose the world—the material world, the world of social relationships—as something that matters to us, often in terms appropriated from that world in uniquely personal ways.

The world within may disclose the world without through its needs, desires, moods, projects and limitations, but it often does so through systems of categorization, description and signification assimilated from the world without. These latter may be imperfect and notable for the slippages and gaps that open up between them and concrete experiences they are called on to conceptualize and convey, but they are nevertheless the means we have at our disposal.

Thus one of the fundamental ideas expressed in many of these essays is that what in everyday experience seem to be the separate worlds of the internal and the external are in fact intertwined and mutually dependent for their meaning. The distinction between myself as a conscious subject and the world around me as an object—a distinction that itself is the more-or-less artificial product of self-conscious reflection—is a secondary event grounded in the primary event of being out in a world that in a sense is at the same time within us.

Consequently, the world for us is a thickly textured, profoundly human one, woven of our material, interpersonal, affective, and imaginative involvements which may be made known to us through the signs, models, material forms, and overall conceptual furniture by which those involvements can be understood, articulated, and conveyed. The world is, to a significant degree, our world, a common world nevertheless assimilated in profoundly personal ways. (This is not to say that something of the non-human world does not escape the human, but that is a topic for another occasion.)

Primary among the means of understanding, articulating and conveying our world are language, gesture, and art. As the philosopher Gianni Vattimo has suggested, it is primarily through art that a particular world can be disclosed, and hence the focus of many of these essays on artworks of various types and disciplines. Improvised music is one particular mode of art that seems especially suited to illustrating the ways in which art as a means of signification can disclose a world; consequently, several of these essays consider improvised music in its existential dimension, which is to say as a meaning-laden, unfolding situation presenting certain possibilities in relation to which we must act on the basis of the choices we must make, in real time. Through those choices and the sounds they give rise to, we disclose ourselves and our ongoing interpretation—of the work-as-situation, of ourselves within that situation.

A very different kind of art frequently visited here is Surreal art, in some of its various forms. In fact, one of the recurring presences haunting these essays is that of André Breton, the founder and chief theorist of Surrealism. Through Breton, Surrealism demonstrated itself to be more than simply a style or movement within art, but rather a stance taken toward the world—as the embodiment and enactment of a certain existential position, in other words. Surrealism not only apprehended the world as something shot through with significance, it committed itself to a position on what that significance would be, and had a deep grasp of some of the internal mechanisms by which this significance was structured.

As Breton put it in his important statement "Marvelous versus Mystery," it would be a significance built on a "compelling and divinatory" sense that, through the kinds of coincidences Breton termed "objective chance" or through the extra-referential, affective associations of words uttered or written in a state of psychic automatism, would reveal one's fate, a fate that wasn't foreordained but rather conditional on one's recognition and free acceptance of it.

Whether or not one accepts the Surrealist worldview—and there are reasons to be skeptical of much in it that was irrational and even plainly superstitious—it does provide a fascinating instance of the articulation of a way of being in the world that read the world as a network of signs and through that reading sought a point at which, again in Breton's words, "the real and the imagined...the communicable and incommunicable" would be reconciled. In other words, As Within, So Without.

Imagining Barnett Newman While Playing Long Tones

The concern with space bores me. I insist on my experience of sensations in time—not the sense of time but the physical sensation of time.
Barnett Newman

Think of a performance on a string instrument consisting of long tones bowed with long pauses in between. Imagine at the same time a typical zip painting by Barnett Newman. A parallel immediately comes to mind: the one structures sound and time in the same way that the other structures the visual field and space.

The parallel emerges most clearly when we think of both in terms of plasticity, that is, in terms of the dynamic relations between and among elements, whether musical on the one hand or pictorial on the other. But first a phenomenological reduction of sorts. Consider Newman's paintings strictly in terms of their structural or compositional qualities, not in terms of the extra-formal associations Newman claimed for them.

The premise is this: the long tone against the audio background is analogous to the zip against the field. The gestalt is somehow similar, even if the tone intervenes in and divides literal time while the zip intervenes and divides pictorial space.

In other words, the zip divides space the way the long bowed tone divides time. Both take place against a background of only apparent emptiness—a background that can stay background or can, through a shift of attention afforded by the work's structure, emerge into and as the foreground. (In fact Newman's negative spaces are painted, and ostensible silence is filled with ambient sound.)

In both the painting and the performance, we encounter the same basic dialectic at work, only couched in different terms: the visual field and the zip; the audio environment and the tone. From this dialectic emerges a distinctive compositional ambiguity.

Start with the painting. The zip establishes the painting's internal relationships—between the painted stripe and the field, between the parts of the field on either side of the zip, between the pictorial space and the edges of the canvas. But it also establishes the painting's external relationships, that is to say the relationships between the painting as an object and the space surrounding it.

The simplicity of the motif and its linear form—the latter drawing the eye beyond the confines of the picture plane (obliquely alluding to the definition of a line as an infinite progression of points extending indefinitely in both directions)—make of the painting less the material representation of something else and more of an independent thing. An object taking its place among a world of objects, in other words.

There is also the matter of rhythm. The zips appear with an imprecise regularity resembling the rhythm of breath.

Consider now the plastic values embodied in the long tone against the pause.

When playing long tones divided by substantial instances of silence, it's natural to hear the focus as falling on the silences, on the open spaces that, inevitably filling with unintended ambient sounds, refuse to stay open. And certainly that is one possible artistic goal of playing music marked by long silences. But here the goal isn't to attempt to illustrate a philosophical point about attentiveness to the ambient sounds surrounding a musical performance—and by extension, one's everyday life—or to point up the ontological reciprocity and interchangeable status linking the intended and unintended sounds in a performance. Rather, it is a formal concern, one which treats negative space as a compositional element pertinent to the performance's overall texture—its episodes of greater or lesser density or intensity, its horizontal and vertical organization, and so forth.

As a formal element silence helps define scale and opens the performance out to engage time.

There is an existential dimension here not to be overlooked. This is time engaged from the lived perspective, the experience of timc in *this* setting by *this* person by virtue of *this* performance. To play a long tone is to divide time in the same way that the line divides the picture plane. To divide time is to establish its scale—to show it as apparently extending indefinitely in either direction. (Whether or not time has an actual beginning and end can be placed in brackets and pushed aside for present purposes.) The sound that divides it is like an opaque finitude inscribed at its center.

The tone dividing time divides audio space. There is the space internal to the performance—the space in which tone is related to tone —and the space external to the performance—the space in which the tone is related to the surrounding audio environment. In the open spaces between its iterations, by not being the environment, the tone negatively defines the boundary—here a very porous one—between the performance and what falls outside of it.

In defining the performance's external relationships this way, the tone points outward to time as a surrounding, infinite field. Just as the zip dividing the field points outward to space as an enfolding state or condition.

Newman's comments, cited above in the epigraph, were made in the context of a set of reflections on aboriginal earthworks he encountered in the Ohio Valley and his being made aware—paradoxically, perhaps—not of space but of time. What Newman seems to have been getting at is the essentially subjective experience of time, its status as a facet of the world as we take it and as we move about through it.

This implies that there is an extent to which time is, for lack of a better term, private. The sensation of time is a function of our interiority at any given moment or span of moments. In comparison to the time shown on a clock—the time passing from second to second at a uniform rate—the sense of time can be dilated, compressed, uneven, suspended, etc., depending on what we are doing or experiencing. Music that seems not to move, whether by virtue of static harmonies or single long-tone melodies, seems to bring the sense of time to a standstill.

Duration becomes something of an image of infinity or eternity until the pause that brings it up short. Hence the function of the pause in reestablishing the sense of scale, of an event taking place against an undifferentiated field. Of raw time.

The length of the tone is judged in relation to the length of the pause. The length of the pause is in turn judged in relation to the length of the tone. An internal relationship of formal elements reciprocally bound. Tone and pause are perceived as relative lengths measured by an internal, variable clock rather than the steady intervals of a timepiece. The subjective experience of time expands and contracts with the bowed tone and with the pauses on either side of the tone.

The way we experience the relationship between the tone and the rest between tones is bound up with anticipation. The tone sounding between rests sets up an expectation—a projection forward to a state in which a subsequently sounding tone will make good on this temporary absence of sound.

In the context of the performance, the absence of the tone implies the recurrence of the tone. Anticipation organizes silence as not-yet-sound.

Thus the effectiveness of the performance inheres in reciprocal expectations: that the tone will fill a silence and that the tone will end and reestablish silence. But sound and silence are unevenly matched—the duration of the tone is finite in principle; the duration of the absence of the tone is in principle infinite. Eventually silence will have the last word and the performance will end. Or be suspended for now, to be taken up later.

As an event of finite duration, the bowed tone inevitably takes on a symbolic function as it comes to represent both the performer and the listener. We are a finitude within time's infinite projection into the future; paradoxically, it's the open nature of the future pulling us forward that anchors a finite existence in time. The bowed tone is metaphorically the carrier wave we ride in that direction.

Until we stop.

Dancing with the Hands

The second movement of the dance begins. Two dancers, a man and a woman, drop to the floor and begin to interact with a miscellany of small objects arranged on the marley before them: found objects, everyday things of various types, unusual objects collected over the years—all objects that had some kind of meaning for their possessors. While the other members of the ensemble continue to move in front of and around them, dancers Shaun English and Micah Trapp pick up, put down, rearrange and otherwise manipulate these things. They do so with a vague air of preoccupation, their attention focused on the things they examine and turn over slowly in their hands, finally putting them down as carefully or as haphazardly as the mood requires.

The name of the piece is *Fossil*; it was performed a few seasons ago by The Nancy Havlik Dance Performance Group. The dance, a semi-improvised piece in which inanimate objects play a significant part, was about the things we collect over time and the meanings they acquire for us.

• • •

Look again at the dancers' hands as they pick up an object, turn it over and then place it back on the marley. At one level this is all that is happening on stage—a dancer is manipulating an object. The movement is natural and self-aware at one and the same time, but the awareness is centered in the body—specifically in the hands and their assured movements. With their hands the dancers project themselves into the surrounding space, organizing it into a situation, a site of given material limits and possibilities in which to act purposefully.

As they do so, they convey a sense of meaning. This is manifested physically. Meaning is externalized in the gesture, carried and conveyed in the sweep of the hand, the pivot of the wrist, the opening and closing of the fingers as they interact with something of mass, with a certain center of gravity, softness or hardness of surface, rigidity or limpness, etc. In essence, the way things are handled is a form of intentionality, a primary or originary form of being directed toward or being about things, as encoded in and communicated by the positions and movements of the body.

This way of being directed toward or about is disclosed by the body's comportment in relation to whatever it is being directed toward. This comportment in turn is permeated by a mood or psychological mode. Think of the adverbs that can be used to describe the body's movement—"rapidly," "sluggishly," "hastily," "thoughtfully," "absently"—all of these tell us something of the movement's psychological grounding, of its being enacted in the context of a mood. The movements of the dancers' hands in *Fossil* can be described as: thoughtful, reflective, absorbed—adverbs conveying the affective side of someone engaged in evaluating the psychological weight of things.

• • •

What then of the objects? Given their mixed provenance, the objects constitute an imperfect network of signification, a miscellany of signs. Some are related to others, some relate to no objects but themselves, but all mean something to someone. A collection of objects brought by one dancer is interconnected by virtue of the relationships of meaning established by that person over time; another person's collection will have its own internal relationships unconnected to any other collection. A relationship of mutual exclusion, that is, until their meeting on the floor and their incorporation into the movements of the dancers' hands. Some of these things are colored by memory, others embody it. The fossils for which the piece was named, collected by Shaun, quite literally embody memory—they are the material signs of vanished organisms.

To the extent that these objects are memory-laden, they carry a twofold layer of meaning. The original encounter with them in the past gave them significance in relation to whatever it was they were needed for at the time; this remembered significance is a kind of foundational meaning for them. And yet the current project—the dance in which they play an important if silent part—brings them forward into the present which imbues them with a significance overlaying their original significance. But to some, they may have no original significance. Consider the dancer handling an object to which she has no historical connection. By virtue of engaging with it in the dance she imbues it with meaning for herself now, in her praxis as solicited by the unfolding performance; to this extent, another meaning comes to the object from the present, and from a person who shares no past with it.

And it really is the dancer's meaning. The individual movements making up this portion of *Fossil* were improvised within the general idea of the piece. Each movement thus represents the dancer's own decision, albeit within the broader framework of the choreographer's general directions. Consequently, the dancers' choices reflect their own individual ways of being among things and of manifesting these things' meanings. Through their individual choices the dancers reveal the underlying meaning of *Fossil*—that the world is known to us not only through thought and perception, but through action and affect.

One of the more subtle turns in the piece is the differential treatment these objects elicit. For example, Micah handles the fossils with care, but not the miscellany of other objects scattered on the floor around her. These different objects solicit different comportments based on the weight or extent of meaning that they have—based, that is, on their intuited value. As Micah's movement shows, significance is a matter of degrees; some objects carry more affective weight than others, some are virtually weightless.

• • •

Movement is an embodied form of intentionality, of which dance is a special case. In an everyday context, movement refers through the body to the world around it in a manner that, for all practical purposes, is non-representational and in fact is prior to what we would recognize as being representational. In the context of dance, though, movement acquires a representational function and in doing so refers to a meaning beyond itself. This opens it up to the question of what it is about, a question that ordinarily wouldn't arise in relation to a movement observed in an everyday context. But in dance, the intentional function of movement becomes explicit and explicitly separable from the physical motion in a way that it normally wouldn't in everyday life. In a sense, through dance, movement becomes conscious of itself as meaningful; it takes on the representational function of being about something in the sense of carrying a meaning to be conveyed through an aesthetically charged medium.

Thus dance is not only the body in its mobility, it is the image of the body in its mobility. It is both movement and the representation of movement all at once. It is simultaneously a first-order phenomenon consisting in the originary mobility of a body defining itself and the world around it, and a second order phenomenon by which that originary mobility becomes an image of itself—a representation of itself—even as it is itself. At one and the same time we are aware of watching the moving body as itself and of watching that same body as the image of its own movement, as the embodied idea of movement.

As Shaun and Micah pick these things up, turn them over in their hands and then put them down again, their hands' movements thus function as gestures of first and second order. The first order is the actual movement of the body organizing its space in real time, that is to say the push of *these* hands against *this* open space or *these* objects. The second order is abstracted from the first, transposing it, as noted, from the plane of movement per se to the plane of movement represented. We go, in other words, from the originary signification of the body as it projects itself into the world to the representation of that projection. The second order is parasitic on and assumes the first order; in a sense, it brings the first order movement to self-awareness.

• • •

Taking up the second-order perspective, when we watch the dancers handling objects we are watching a process of evaluation, of meaning explicitly given and taken, and held up to view. The fact of the performance acts as a framework or boundary marking the demarcation between simply picking up and manipulating an object and representing the picking up and manipulating of an object; the representational capacity of the movement thus arises in the gap between the everyday conveyance of meaning and the recreation of that conveyance in the context of a performance. Here manipulation refers to itself, intends itself as both the starting point and the endpoint of action or gesture.

This second-order representation of movement is, for lack of a better term, expressive. It pushes to the foreground the affective aspect or mood through which the objects' significances are disclosed. Thus what the movement in *Fossil* ultimately is about—what it is meant to capture or reproduce—is the way a person projects out into the world and in fact is out into the world, as a giver of meaning colored with affect. The affect that saturates *Fossil* is a composite of memory and loss. This is a mood facilitated by a certain withdrawal from the present, a withdrawal into the objects as they're handled and explored for their meanings. The dancers signal this mood through the movement of their hands but also in their facial expressions as configured in a certain distraction or apparent disengagement with the present moment—the past being a screen shrouding the present and blurring its edges with the superimposed figures of things remembered.

The world is a network of significances, a quasi-geological formation whose strata are the things and their meanings that we and others have put there. In representing the network of significances these things embody, *Fossil* is the world in microcosm.

Free Improvisation & How It Means

Does free improvisation mean anything? This may seem like a strange question to ask. Surely when we play a musical free improvisation there must be something meaningful that we're doing. There is, but to push the question a little farther in, what is it that we mean, and how do we mean it?

Free improvisation is an activity. Like any activity it has a meaning which derives from the kind of activity it is and from the way it engages the person undertaking it. Free improvisation is a creative activity, one which results in the creation of an artwork, no matter how ephemeral. The improvised performance may literally vanish into air once it's completed, but even if it exists only as a temporary object, during that time it carries and conveys meaning, the meaning put there by the improvisers.

It just seems essential to an artwork, of which a freely improvised performance is one, that it mean something. By one definition, an artwork is something that represents an intended meaning in a medium-specific way. Consequently the meaning of an artwork—a painting, a poem, a piece of music composed or improvised—inheres in its representation of content—that is, in its capacity to be about something. What makes it an artwork as opposed to a more mundane representational entity—such as, say, a street sign—is the role its medium plays in conveying, and indeed in constituting, its content as such. Thus for an artwork it isn't just a matter of what it represents, but of how it represents, that constitutes its meaning. Its medium is, to a significant extent, its meaning.

If when we talk of what an artwork means, we're referring to its content, or what the work is about, we might further think of this content as having two components, one of which is medium-independent, and the other of which is inextricable from its medium. Each of these two components is deeply intertwined with the other, but still, it's possible to speak of each separately and in its own terms.

The central, medium-independent content of free improvisation is the improviser's disclosure of him- or herself, from the first person perspective. When we play a free improvisation, we relate something very basic about ourselves, from our own point of view. What we play relates our own interpretation of the given moment, how we see it and how and to what extent we commit ourselves to it. To a degree greater than with any other type of musical performance, the meaning of free improvisation inheres in just this conveyance of the performer's own perspective on the music. It is about what it is like to participate in the music in the moment it's being created. This is an interpretive meaning. Not the performer's interpretation of the score—because of course there is no score--but an interpretation of the performance as it unfolds.

As an art concerned with self-disclosure, free improvisation is essentially expressive. It externalizes, in a medium-specific form, the emotional and cognitive states of the improviser as they pertain to the performance unfolding in the moment. The key idea here is "expression." The underlying intuition is that free improvisation doesn't describe or depict the performer's state, it *expresses* that state. What this means is that in creating a free improvisation, we aren't purporting to depict something as we would in telling a story or describing an event or painting a picture or sculpting a figure. Instead, expression through improvisation is a kind of modeling or simulation rather than a variety of depiction.

Think of how music can convey an emotion such as agitation. With rapid flurries of notes, loud dynamics and dissonant pitch combinations, it can model the restlessness and unease of an agitated emotional state. And no doubt we can imagine ways in which music models other kinds of emotional states—quiet, long tones for serenity, for example, or as in the Baroque era, the use of the minor key to convey emotional gravity. What seems to be involved here is a kind of simulation in which certain features or qualities of something are represented in a different medium by way of features or qualities appropriate to that medium. The central notion here is again that of representation, or something standing for something else—specifically, of musical features modeling emotional states or impulses. In free improvisation what is being represented is the state of the improviser, the first person perspective on the performance, in the medium of organized sound. Sound, organized by the performer in such a way, stands for his or her state in relation to the performance.

Expression of the first person perspective through modeling of emotional states is something done to brilliant effect by, for example, some of the more unrestrained free jazz performances of the 1960s. But free improvisation can of course also be about things other than the emotional impulses or moods experienced at the moment of improvisation. It can be about the interrelationships among the performers, or—and this is to anticipate somewhat—it can be about the interplay of musical elements, in which the musicians are engaged in contributing complementary or contrasting formal structures in building the performance. Even so, it would seem that the modeling of the performer's emotional responses to the unfolding performance is something fundamental and always there, whether in the foreground as the main substance of what is being expressed, or alternately as a kind of shading or coloring of the main substance of what is being expressed. It is there in the same way that a non-reflective awareness of or presence to self is fundamental and always there when we engage in purposive action. The parallel is perhaps a rough one, but suggestive nevertheless.

Expression to Description: The Move from the First to the Third Person Perspective

The expressive part of free improvisation's content can be described —we can say of a player that his line is agitated or her harmonies are anxious—but in itself it isn't description. Through the agitated line or anxious harmonies the performer isn't describing his or her state but rather is expressing it. In this case it might be useful to think of the difference between description and expression as corresponding roughly to the difference between the third-person and first-person perspectives, respectively. Or, as a kind of paraphrase.

In fact, one way to think of medium-independent meaning generally is to think of it as liable to paraphrase or description in another medium, most typically language. Thus what we can paraphrase about an artwork's meaning is, briefly, what we can describe in terms that aren't medium-specific or peculiar to the artwork. We can, for example, paraphrase the content of a poem in prose, can describe in words the story or event depicted in a painting or the figure or geometrical form depicted in a sculpture.

With free improvisation this matter of paraphrase becomes complicated. To see why, first consider instead a piece of program music that purports to depict or comment on something in the world. A work like Sean McClowry's *April '94* for double bass and electronics specifically alludes to events in the Balkans in 1994; it is, in a broad sense, descriptive, and what it describes can be paraphrased. But what of music that isn't program music, that is to say, music whose content isn't descriptive by intent? It still can be described—still can be paraphrased—but taking the descriptive stance toward it requires a shift in perspective that—crucially—is not the performer's perspective. In paraphrasing we move from the first person perspective to a third person perspective. Through the third person perspective we can describe the content we perceive in the improvised performance in a way that the performer, expressing it from within the first person perspective, quite naturally does not. A kind of translation, in a sense, is required—and which is appropriate in that paraphrase itself also is a kind of translation—which like any translation can be more or less accurate, more or less literal or imaginative.

Form as Expression

It seems intuitive to hold that the meaning of free improvisation—its serving as a vehicle for the self-disclosure of the improviser—is to be found in the content it expresses through the kind of modeling suggested above, and which can be paraphrased through the third person perspective. But what of the medium? What, or how does it contribute to the expression of meaning, specifically to the expression of self-disclosure?

What's left of the work after the medium-independent content has been extracted, as it were, is the formal language in which that content is presented: the rhythms and diction of the poem, the visual composition and literal colors of the painting, etc. Any formal language includes an expressive element, but with free improvisation, the expressive element is particularly important—in fact, we wouldn't be far off in saying that in free improvisation, form just is expression.

In the absence of pre-conceived or composed forms, a free improvisation's forms and sounds are all chosen by the performers, in real time. Consequently, as free improvisers, we don't realize or replicate another's pre-existing, formal language—or if we do we can only do so imperfectly, because we are not that other person—but instead express our own. In doing so, we disclose something substantial about ourselves—specifically, our internalized sense of forms and their appropriate uses. Thus formal choices—what it is we actually play in real time—say something about us as realized possibilities within the context of the purposive activity that is free improvisation. As such, they supply a substantial part of the improvisation's overall meaning.

Because these formal choices reflect our ongoing judgment in real time (albeit a judgment made more often than not tacitly or without prior or explicit reflection), they effectively express our cognitive responses to the performance. They give signs, in organized sound, of how things are with us as we assimilate and respond to the ongoing flow of musical cues and forms. In this sense, the forms we create are indicative, in an expressive way, of one very important dimension of our first person perspective on the performance.

Thus our freely improvised formal choices do a kind of double duty. In the first place, they are the means through which we disclose our first person stance—they are the medium through which we express our position within the flow of sound. But at the same time they are in themselves meaningful as the expression of our formal judgments. These latter count as simply another dimension or facet of how things are with us during the course of the performance. It just follows, then, that the way musical content is presented—the formal elements and relationships through which its content is conveyed—is part of that content. These formal elements and relationships are part of content, part of meaning.

A Mediated Immediacy

Free improvisation has sometimes been characterized as a music of immediacy—of the direct expression of the artist's state of being. And to an extent this is true. But no matter how immediate it might appear, what we express through free improvisation is in fact mediated—through the musical gestures, forms and structures we have learned, the technical competence we have acquired and the limitations that constrain us, which provide the representational means for what it is that we express through them. To the extent that the free improvisation is a musical performance, it is bound up in this system of representations which mediate, and consequently give form to, the expression of how things are with the musician at any given moment of the improvisation.

As with other artworks, then, when we convey meaning through free improvisation we are doing it through a system of representation. This may seem odd, since music is not ordinarily thought of as being representational in the same sense that a painting depicting an event or a person, or a sentence expressing a proposition, is representational. And in a sense the question of whether or not free improvisation is representational is a special case of the larger question of whether or not music can be representational. Although music doesn't represent what it is about in the same way that a descriptive painting or a proposition represents what it is about, it is nevertheless representational in that it uses a medium—sound organized into formal structures, no matter how informal they may initially strike our ears—to convey, that is to represent, a meaning. It just follows that free improvisation, as a variety of music, entails a kind of expression that is mediated representationally by the forms, gestures and formal elements through which its meaning is conveyed.

But while I believe this is true—that free improvisation is a representationally mediated art form—paradoxically, I think that it is in some valid, intuitive sense immediate in that the state of the performer and his or her own choices of sounds and gestures provide the primary meaning of the art form, as opposed to pre-conceived or composed forms. Its primary meaning is the expression of what I've termed the first person perspective, albeit through the medium of musical forms and structures.

So then yes, the meaning of free improvisation is mediated, but the sense of urgency, the reliance on moment-to-moment choice—in short, the risks of working without a net so critical to the actual doing of free improvisation—give it an experiential immediacy that is there for us to hear.

And To Improvise Is Human

In the remarks above, free improvisation and how it means have been considered from the point of view of what an individual improviser may be conveying, as an individual. But there is as well a larger, more general sense in which the meaning of free improvisation serves as a kind condensed symbol of human life which—like an improvisation--often seems to be a more or less extemporized response to one unexpected set of circumstances after another, a sequence of instant replies to whatever happens to be thrown our way. Seen from this broader perspective, free improvisation presents an image of life dramatized, radicalized and condensed: precisely to the extent that it just is a moment of life put under pressure by our having been thrown into an artificial or ritualized situation in which time is compressed and we must act now, immediately, on the basis of whatever the situation has to offer us.

But there's a deeper, more fundamental sense in which improvisation crystallizes and symbolizes the human situation. Both share a basic structure that can properly be characterized as existentially primary—that is, both begin with a lack or need in response to which we are thrust out into a situation in which we must act on the basis of the possibilities open to us. The freely improvised performance emblematizes this lack by starting literally with nothing: with a zero moment defined by the non-being of the performance that is to take place. The zero moment is a suspended moment in which action is pure imminence. At this zero moment, the improviser is thrown into—*chooses* to be thrown into—a situation that demands action in order that he or she bring about a desired future state—a realized piece of music—that, not incidentally, isn't guaranteed to succeed. At its heart is a lack—the lack of the desired object. In this case the object lacking isn't a thing out there in the world ready to be obtained, but instead is a piece of music that has no existence prior to its being played. Not only is the desired object lacking, but so too is any pre-existing structure, such as a score or other compositional framework, out of which the object can be made. The object is its own objective: not a thing per se, but a process of invention and creation the end result of which will be a finished performance. Which has yet to be created. This lack of a performance is the immediate motivation for the performance, something like a provocation that pushes one out from the stillness of the zero moment in order to commence the gestures, actions and realized choices that put the music in action.

The initial choice of what to play, the leap into action from the zero moment, begins the improvisation. It also initiates a pattern of action that, far from being unique to improvisation, is paradigmatic of human action generally. That pattern consists in the pursuit of a course of action aimed at obtaining something that will make good a lack or meeting a need—a pattern anthropologist Walter Burkert in his book *Structure and History in Greek Mythology and Ritual* has described with the infinitive verb phrase "to get."

In the case of a free improvisation, in which a musical work or performance is brought into being seemingly out of nothing, we could substitute the infinitive "to make" for Burkert's "to get." Such a substitution represents a simple transposition to an analogous term rather than a substantial change of conceptual key, since the underlying pattern undergoes no change. In both cases, something lacking or desired is procured through our action. In a sense, "to make" is just a variation on "to get" or, if we take "to get" as the more encompassing or general term, "to make" is a particular case of "to get." But there is this difference: when the action is "to make," the object to be obtained or "gotten" isn't something that exists prior to our obtaining it but rather has to be made by us in order for it to be gotten: the getting, in other words, is in the making. And in the making, the basic human action pattern is reenacted. At its core, then, a free improvisation is never merely a purely musical event; it is a quintessentially human event.

The Angel of Contingency

A New Angel

It isn't very large. At 31.8 x 24.2 centimeters, Paul Klee's *Angelus Novus*, an oil-transfer drawing produced in 1920, is only a little bigger than a standard 8.5" x 11" piece of paper. Nor is the picture's image particularly elaborate. It consists of a single figure apparently floating in a void. The figure is almost a doodle—a line drawing of an oddly hybrid creature with human and avian features.

The title of the piece identifies the figure as an angel—a "new angel." Its novelty consists in part in its strangeness. Klee's angel defies popular conventions of what an angel is supposed to look like. It isn't especially elegant or graceful, or endowed with the slender ethereality one might expect of an angel. Instead, we find a rather strangely proportioned, thinly-rendered creature with a blocky physique facing us with a bland expression and eyes looking slightly to the side and past us. The wings are thrown upward; they are thick and resemble arms more than anything, particularly since they culminate in what clearly appear to be hands held open and flat beside the figure's head. The legs are unmistakably bird legs; a curving, vaguely triangular form at the bottom of the angel's torso could be either the end of a skirted garment or a bird's tail. The angel's hair is tightly curled, giving him a curious resemblance to Harpo Marx, whose time was yet to come when Klee's work was created. And unlike the silent Marx the open-mouthed angel appears to have been caught in the act of speaking. This is the most angelic thing about him.

By virtually any standard, *Angelus Novus* would be considered a minor work. But its peculiar history of ownership has made it perhaps one of Klee's best-known and most-discussed works. The picture was purchased in 1921 by essayist Walter Benjamin, for whom it inspired a famous paragraph in his set of aphoristic, fragmentary "Theses on the Philosophy of History," which were completed shortly before his death by suicide in 1940. The circumstances surrounding the theses' writing and completion gave them a poignancy and pathos that couldn't help but reflect back onto the interpretation Benjamin made of Klee's angel. For Benjamin, Klee's *Angelus Novus* was the Angel of History, a horrified figure turning his back to the future and facing the past in order to bear witness to History, which Benjamin characterized as "one single catastrophe." For Benjamin, whom many saw as a martyr to that same History, Klee's almost childishly depicted angel turns deeply tragic, its insubstantial form taking on the weight of History as a leaden, recurring nightmare of violence and destruction in an eternal cycle—an eschatology without an exit.

Although Benjamin's reading of the Klee drawing was highly influential, it represented an arbitrary flight of the imagination. There's nothing in the picture to suggest that the angel is reacting to a disaster; his posture and expression don't seem to signal horror, and the surrounding void he occupies gives no evidence of the wreckage wrought by human action taking place in time. Instead, Klee's angel seems to have served as a kind of open variable that could take any value, or a blank page on which could be written any narrative. The picture's very sketchiness could be argued to have done much to license an imaginative interpretation. The angel is a figure without a context—ironically, in light of Benjamin's reading, it is a figure without a visible history. He is lacking any surrounding objects or depicted events or supporting symbols or any other kind of iconography that could establish some sense of a narrative. There is nothing in the picture except a strange being that itself seems strangely balanced between avian and anthropic forms. This isn't to say that Klee's image shuts down any attempt at interpretation; it's clearly labeled as an angel, and is shown doing something that is hinted at from its posture and expression. Look at him and he looks back, at once obliquely and absently. Most significantly, though, his mouth is open, as if he's about to speak or has been caught in mid-speech.

What Is New Is What Is Old

In depicting his angel as speaking or about to speak, Klee at least tacitly acknowledges the angel's traditional function as messenger. This function is encoded in the DNA of the word "angel": etymologically it derives from the Greek "ángelos" ("ἁγγελος")—literally, "messenger." By itself, the word's Greek prehistory implies nothing of the divine, but in naming the function it implies a relationship of intermediation. The messenger is a kind of third term between two others, an intermediary or go-between relating the message's sender to its receiver. This intermediary function speaks directly to the matter of the bridging nature of the angel's status as a divinity; it is precisely as a divine being that the angel mediates between the human and divine worlds. The carrier of messages from the divine to the human serves as a bridge anchored in the former, and it is this anchor that provides the ground for the possibility of the angel's function as messenger.

The angel as we know it has significant precedent in, and to an extent is prefigured by, the Greek figures of Hermes and Iris. Both served as the gods' heralds and were given the title of ἁγγελος; they set the template for the angel as a means of transmission between two worlds. A more direct prefiguration of the angel may be found in the daemon which, by contrast to the gods Hermes and Iris was considered a minor or lesser deity. The daemon was a sometimes ill-defined element in Classical ontotheology, but as a lesser divinity it did play a mediating role between the human and the divine. As it appeared from Homer forward, the daemon was something of a multivalent being. A daemon could represent a god's intervention in human affairs when undertaken in a certain obscuring manner, or it could represent an honored person's status after death. From Plato onward, though, the daemon begins to look more specifically angelic as it takes on the role of a guardian or tutelary being. In Book X of the *Republic*, Plato describes the daemon as a kind of benevolent bridge between the human and divine; the third century Neoplatonist Plotinus adds the crucial point that these intermediary beings speak with voices.

Klee's figure of the Angelus Novus, with its brusquely outlined form, lacks volume and heft. Its bodily insubstantiality recalls Plotinus' bodily insubstantial yet still material beings. If the daemon represents the prehistory of the angel—if the daemon is, in effect, the reverse to the angel's obverse, a reverse made a reverse precisely for the historical and theological reasons that have been buried or elided—one can follow Klee's line and imagine it connecting the angel to its daemonic ancestor. Klee's image seems to illustrate the outcome of a process of refiguration and distortion through which genealogy is both obscured and carried forward in still-recognizable form. The very pseudo-primitive way in which the Angelus Novus is portrayed is in effect an invitation to recall the angel's origins and to see it as one in a complementary pair of inseparable elements that both illuminate and obscure each other. What is new about the Angelus Novus is what is old: the traces of its history made visible.

The Angel's Alterity

As an intermediary between the human and divine worlds, the angel bears a functional resemblance to the oracle. Not only are both figures purported to be go-betweens, but the kinds of mediation both provide are closely akin. They both serve as channels of communication linking the two worlds; specifically, as conduits of directed messages. But where the oracle is caught in an ontological dilemma—she is human and thus by nature is limited by the finitude of human mortality while being at the same time at least provisionally and temporarily granted a vision of the god's perspective of eternity—the angel is not. It is a divine being, even if of a lower or inferior order. It may share in some human traits, but in the final calculation it is other than human. Its relationship to the human world is one of alterity in spite of its being, like the daemon, susceptible to human impulses and affections.

The Angelus Novus, with its strange mixture of human and avian features, casts the angel's alterity with hybrid qualities peculiar to Klee's way of imagining them. His angel embodies its alterity in an explicit, if—assuming that the avian takes on a symbolic weight to the extent that bird flight is analogous to the upward pull of the divine or the intelligible—indirect, manner. In fact its peculiarity is its alterity. In its ontological undecidability, in its neither-this-nor-that, it is both itself—whatever we may think "itself" is—and not itself. Neither human nor avian, neither corporeal nor ethereal. Like an angel or daemon it seems to be pulled in both directions: upward, by its outspread wings, or downward, to settle on its bird feet.

An Annunciation

Its ontological strangeness aside, the action the Angelus Novus is engaged in is clear. He is speaking, or is about to speak. Does his face provide any clues as to the nature of the speech? Possibly. His expression seems to signal preoccupation or absorption in something other than the interlocutor presumably standing before him (standing, conveniently enough, in the place where the viewer is standing). At least it seems that way, given his posture of facing the viewer/interlocutor full on while directing his eyes slightly to the side—out of modesty, timidity, or an attentiveness to what he's saying, we don't know. But it does look like the kind of expression someone making a recitation might wear. We could reasonably speculate that he's making an announcement—and it's true that Klee's angel, with his bland, open-mouthed look, bears more of a resemblance to the Angel of the Annunciation than to a horrified Angel of History.

What is it that Klee's angel could be announcing? We don't know, and it's really impossible to say. The rest of the picture provides no context, and therefore no clues. In this secular age we could imagine that he's announcing that there is no announcement other than news of the withdrawal of the divine and the abandonment of human being to its own care and its own meaning. With the withdrawal of the metaphysical ground of the divine—or any other transcendent order, for that matter—the human self-understanding of its place in the world would be a matter of self-generated meaning. Or rather of meaning self-conscious of its self-generation and thus aware of its situation within the moving current of ongoing interpretation.

The Ground Is an Abyss

Whatever the specific message we may want to attribute to Klee's angel, its epiphenomenal or meta-meaning will be marked by a certain incommensurability. Incommensurability may not be the meaning of the message itself, but it is an inseparable quality of that meaning, a meaning-within-the-meaning that the message brings along with it like a stone within a fruit. This incommensurability just is a consequence of the angel's ontological status vis-à-vis human being. Divine beings, even of a lesser or inferior kind, would be presumed to participate in what could be characterized as a pure example of the so-called metaphysics of (epistemological) presence in that the intelligible forms or essences of things would be immediately present to them.

This presence just is a consequence of their access to the intelligible world—the world of the pure universal or enduring Being in which beings are known in their fullness and actual reality, undiminished by decay in time or by the other imperfections inherent in the material world of transience and appearance. This transcendent world is, like the divine of which it is supposed to be a manifestation, the condition for the possibility of the angel's being. It is, in other words, one of the fundamental rules constituting any framework in which such divinities can play a role; it is by that token the ground and source of their function as messenger or herald.

Intelligible form is located nowhere in the material world itself but nevertheless pervades it everywhere, like a higher dimension imperceptible to the three dimensional world of everyday human habitation. It is through the ambassadorship of the angel that this world discloses itself as an opening out of itself to the human world—an opening that is transmitted with the angel's message.

At the same time, though, the content of this intelligible world is ineffable and incommunicable within the limits of human language. Limit is a feature of human language; meaning often escapes it, communicative intentions may be in part opaque to it, and in any event it cannot claim direct contact with any purported extra-linguistic essences. In contrast to the pure Idea or essence, human language doesn't point directly to naturally occurring categories but instead organizes and simplifies reality in often arbitrary or pragmatic ways. Thus what the angel presumably is privy to is incommensurable with the language he would be compelled to use in communicating it to the human recipient.

There is consequently a communicative gap here that cannot be bridged except with provisional materials and partial results. The point at which the angel's message enters human language is thus a point of slippage and expediency, of inconsistency and coarse reduction, of incompletion and partiality. To the extent that the meaning of the angel's message is purported to be divinely inspired and to have originated in the intelligible world, his annunciation announces nothing so much as its incompleteness or inadequacy to itself.

Thus if Klee's angel's eyes are averted it may be out of embarrassment over the realization that the bridge between the divine and the human that he represents is built over an abyss.

The Angel of Contingency

Klee's angel speaks, but as he does so, does he know that his message is a compromise between the Ideal nature of its originary intention and the arbitrary and partial nature of its vehicle in human language? That, as a compromise, it is compromised as well? And would it matter if he did? What if, instead of taking him as a symbol of language's ability or inability to transmit a communicative intention we take him instead as a symbol of language in its contingency—in its use at *this* given moment, in *this* given situation? Granted, it's highly unlikely that Klee's small drawing carries any such intended meaning. But it just is in the nature of a symbol to point beyond itself, to meanings both intended and—sometimes as in cases like this, where the iconography can reasonably be seen to license it—penumbral.

In simultaneously heralding the presence of the messenger and greeting the recipient of the message the annunciation, as the initiating moment of a relationship between interlocutors, is the exemplary moment in which the angel's function as intermediary is focused and dramatized. For if it is the function of the angel to act as a vessel of communication, he must first make himself known by calling out to the recipient of the message and in doing so open up a channel of transmission. The seemingly simple greeting represents a complex moment within the communicative relationship: at once a confrontation and an acknowledgement, it initiates an encounter that opens a mutually defined space shared by the bearer and the receiver of the message that is about to follow.

The greeting is only one moment—the first moment—within the larger event of speech that it initiates. The instance of speech is a contingent, essentially existential relationship between interlocutors taking place on the ground of language. Speech is an event of language, embodied in the instance of speaking, as well as a conveyance of meaning; by virtue of its being such an event it creates an opening in which the speaker and listener can coexist as possibilities for each other: possibilities of understanding or misunderstanding, of concord or discord, of cooperation or opposition, of concern or indifference. All of these possibilities are structured by the contingent circumstances of each party to the event, who stand over against and with each other within this common opening. Over and beyond its constituent elements of intention, meaning and reception, the event of speech, and by extension of language, is about *this* communicative relationship entered into by *these* participants.

In portraying the angel in the act of speaking, Klee's *Angelus Novus* exemplifies and emblematizes the taking place of language as the opening to a purely contingent, existential event that both surpasses and encompasses the apparently simple act of transmitting a message. To the extent that he can serve as such an emblem, Klee's angel reveals himself to be the Angel of Contingency.

Writing Pushed Beyond Writing

The god whose oracle is in Delphi neither indicates clearly nor conceals, but gives a sign. Heraclitus

Since the late 1990s a form of visual poetry consisting in works that resemble, mimic, or otherwise allude to writing systems but that are not in fact examples of any conventionally known writing system, have been much in evidence. These wordless writings—texts or quasi-texts that work outside of systems of ordinary language—*qua* objects inhabit a unique ontological borderland between writing and visual art. Poet Jim Leftwich in the late 1990s coined the expression "asemic text" to describe these hybrid objects. "Asemic" literally means "without meaning;" asemic texts (or more broadly, compositions) can be further defined as examples of a kind of creative writing that employs linguistic or quasi-linguistic elements or marks—letters, symbols and characters taken from actual or invented writing systems; cursive lines and other gestural marks suggesting handwriting, and so forth—for aesthetic or expressive purposes rather than for communicating messages with a pre-given, author-produced semantic content. The asemic text, in other words, lacks deliberate signification; poet Tim Gaze summed it up neatly when he stated that asemic texts carry no "writer-intended meaning."

To be sure, works that we would now recognize as asemic texts or compositions had been created years before Leftwich named them as such. The well-known paintings resembling scribbles on a blackboard had been produced by artist Cy Twombly since the 1960s; more ancient roots can be traced back to the illegible calligraphy of Tang

Dynasty poet Zhang Xu and the 19th century Zen-inspired calligraphy of no-mind. Another, seemingly unlikely, precursor may be the as-yet undeciphered Voynich Manuscript—if in fact it is the undecipherable hoax or parody many think it is, rather than an actual communication in a secret language.

Because asemic texts mimic some of the salient formal properties of actual, contentful written texts, they are fascinating not only for their appearance—and consequently for their inherent aesthetic value as visual compositions—but for the ways that they engage, by way of negation, questions of meaning and interpretation. Here I will follow the way of negation to see where it leads and to find out what its implications are for meaning and for the very possibility of meaning. Except as it relates directly to these matters, the formal aspect of asemic writing I will leave for consideration for some other time.

The Way of Negation

If asemic compositions mimic the salient formal properties of conventional texts, they do so without containing or conveying meaning in a way that conventional texts ordinarily would. Unlike conventional, semantically encumbered texts, asemic texts refuse to indicate a determinate object, event, idea, action or other extra-linguistic referent. As with abstract paintings, to which they often bear a striking resemblance, asemic compositions' content is the product of their formal elements and relationships, while their expressive impact consists in the associations those elements and relationships give rise to in the viewer. The formal makeup of an asemic composition may entice us into thinking that we are confronting a message conveyed by real linguistic signs with a semantic function, but when we look more closely we find that these signs are in fact empty ciphers signifying nothing in particular. We can examine them and interrogate them as much as we like, but they can't be made to divulge secrets they aren't in fact keeping. Our initial impressions aside, these signs reveal themselves to be quasi-signs that fall into no recognizable, and thus conventionally decodable, linguistic patterns.

And yet their emptiness does signify something after all. Their refusal of semantics—their refusal to have the text refer, based on an author-intended meaning—negatively discloses the semantic dimension of language through its very negation. Negating language's semantic function serves only to dramatize the fact that referring is one of language's essential functions: its absence tells us that it is missing because it is something we anticipate will be there, but in fact is not there. In mimicking the forms while vacating the content of writing, the asemic text sets up an obstacle that abruptly jolts us out of our usual expectation—a complacent expectation, as the rudeness of the jolt makes all too clear—that where there is a written text, there necessarily is an intended meaning. The way of negation, in other words, is the way of alienation—of alienating language from its ordinary function of reference.

The asemic composition's alienation of language comes by way of its illegibility. Illegibility is its fundamental property; it is also the instrument by which it severs the connection between writing as such and writing's ordinary function of conveying information in the shape of a message we can decode. The asemic composition's illegibility defamiliarizes writing by forcing attention to turn to the sensual facts on the page—the shapes of the letters and/or other constituent signs, the continuity and rhythms of the line, and so forth. When used as vehicles to transmit meaning, these contingencies of typography or calligraphy ordinarily take on a virtual invisibility, as the meaning of the message acts like a kind of solvent that erodes the sensual facts of writing and leaves behind nothing but itself. (Thus the way of negation is also the way of de-dissolution, as the absence of meaning allows the sensual facts of language to precipitate back into view.) With meaning subtracted from the writing there is no remainder but these sensual facts, which by virtue of their functionlessness become an alien presence.

In its own way, the asemic composition would seem to resemble nothing so much as the philosopher Giorgio Agamben's account, in *Language and Death: the Place of Negativity*, of the "pure voice." Inspired by Augustine and the medieval grammarians, Agamben describes the pure voice as a kind of pure self-presence of language devoid of determinate content: an empty and yet latent demonstration that "language is taking place here" (p. 34), an event that erupts in the moment that the voice sounds and before the question of its meaning arises. The pure voice is more than simply the sound of the voice—it is as well the anticipation of what that sound will signify. The pure voice appears at the moment in which spoken language surges up as a simple self-presence in which a "pure intention to signify…is given… before a determinate event of meaning is produced" (p. 33). The pure voice, in other words, is the event of language itself as embodied in the physical act of speaking. It is an event made known to the speaker through the speaker's self-presence *qua* speaker in the act of speaking —not through the content of what is spoken. If we were to describe the phenomenological aspect of the pure voice it would simply be as what it is like to enunciate X, where X is a variable standing for whatever intended meaning is being spoken. The actual value for X—the actual content of what is spoken—does not come into play in the pure voice; rather, the pure voice is the physical presence of spoken language as the "bearer of some [as yet] unknown meaning" (p. 33).

The asemic text, as the physical record of the gestures that left their marks on paper, represents a "pure writing" that serves as the written counterpart of the pure voice. Just as the pure voice, as the physical self-presence of the speaker engaged in the act of speaking, embodies the event of language while parenthesizing and putting out of play the matter of content, so the marks in asemic writing serve as the traces of the self-presence of the writer *qua* writer in the physical act of writing —before the question of meaning can arise. But because as far as the asemic text is concerned the question of intended meaning is prevented from arising at all, that same text remains at the moment of pure writing—remains, in other words, fixed at that point before the question of meaning arises. To that extent, the asemic composition conveys the simple and immediate message, "writing is taking place here." As with pure voice, the asemic composition signifies that zero point or nothingness that separates the material vehicle of language from the fixed content it ordinarily carries. In the case of the asemic composition, though, that moment when determinate meaning finally does arise would seem to be perpetually put off.

Lack of intended meaning is to the asemic text what latency is to the pure voice—an emptiness that reveals something that ordinarily would be there or should be there. If the pure voice illuminates a clearing in which meaningful speech will arise, the lack of an intended meaning at the heart of the asemic text is, conversely, like a dark light throwing into sharp relief the fact that ordinary texts do in fact carry an intended meaning. To chase this observation further—to chase it into the area of metaphysics, in fact—the asemic text's lack of intended meaning corresponds to the unspeakability of ultimate being in neo-Platonic and other ontotheologies of late antiquity. If, as according to these ontotheologies the ultimate ground of being is a nothingness that can only be spoken with the voice of silence, then similarly, the ground of linguistic meaning in the intention-to-mean can be conveyed through its negation. In either case we are confronted by a paradox: what is either unreachable or refused is revealed precisely by virtue of its being unreachable or refused.

The Impossibility of the Asemic & Homo interpretans

But are asemic compositions truly empty of meaning? Are they in fact asemic? From the beginning the name was understood to be paradoxical if not outright contradictory. Leftwich, in a 27 January 1998 letter to Gaze, acknowledged that "[a]n asemic text…might be involved with units of language for reasons other than that of producing meaning [and thus] would seem to be an ideal, an impossibility, but possibly worth pursuing for just that reason." By 2011 Leftwich refined his initial insight to include the caveat that "there is no such thing as asemic anything. everything is readable, i.e., can be and will be given meaning."

The impossibility of the asemic is in fact an appropriate point of departure. The intuition that that realization encapsulates is that meaning must always be made present, particularly in texts and other objects that appear as ordered collections of signs of whatever sort. Meaning doesn't vacate the locus of the sign any more than we can abandon the possibility of meaning in anything that, whether designated specifically with that function or not, can be interpreted as a sign.

We turn to the possibility of meaning—to the idea that this mark here has something to convey to us—almost reflexively. If we naturally take the world to be something that has something to say to us if only we knew how to decrypt its message, then our adopting an interpretive stance toward things in the world—particularly those that have the distinguishing look of signs—will be second nature.

The interpretive stance is natural to us as beings inhabiting a meaning-saturated world. Human being is *homo interpretans*, the being that interprets, and meaning is always a possibility to a being that is prone to interpret. To *homo interpretans* text in general, and a quasi-text made up of marks and signs that mimic rather than instantiate a known writing system in particular, are naturally prone to holding out the possibility of meaning, and thus of soliciting interpretation.

We might say that, like the Delphic oracle the asemic text neither indicates clearly nor conceals, but instead gives a sign. A sign that it falls to the querant—here, the reader—to perceive and interpret.

For *homo interpretans*, the question isn't whether or not interpretation will take place, but how. If there is a devil hiding here, he is to be found in the details of that how. And there can be many devils, which is to say many modes of interpretive stances one can take, given the type of meaning one expects to find. This latter may be, for example, indicative—denoting or referring to some object, event or idea, real or fictional; expressive—i.e., articulating a psychological state or feeling; performative—i.e., accomplishing something rather than alluding to it or describing it. Our stance toward any one of these types of meaning will reflect the appropriate response to the meaning in question—looking for the truth or accuracy or similitude or self-consistency of the indicative; being affected by the expressive; deriving pleasure from or being moved by the aesthetic, and so on. More generally, if to interpret some text X is to understand X as containing some sort of meaning, then this expected meaning serves as the criterion one uses for choosing an interpretive stance. For conventional texts whose intended meanings can be gleaned from formal features or contextual cues, settling on the appropriate interpretive stance is in principle something that can be done with reasonable confidence. With an asemic text, this confidence breaks down.

While the meaning of even the most conventional text will be marked by some degree of ambiguity or indeterminacy, the type of meaning we expect from it will, at least initially, establish a more-or-less generally understood framework of reference that places certain constraints on what counts as the "right," or at least plausible, interpretation. But because the asemic text lacks originary meaning, it lacks such an initially graspable framework and attendant set of constraints. To interpret the asemic text is to grasp negatively the very taking place of meaning. The place language opens up for meaning is, in the asemic text, indicated by the effective absence of intended meaning, thus making of that place a vacancy; absence of meaning functions as a placeholder or a sign reading "here (would) be meaning."

Interpretation must somehow fill that vacancy, but in order that it do so, the most appropriate interpretive stance must be taken up.

For a clue to what that stance will be, consider that with no referential content to dominate it, the aesthetic itself in effect becomes the asemic work's message. It is, in effect, essentially an aesthetic object. And as an aesthetic object the asemic text overflows the category "written text" and spills over into the category to which abstract drawings and paintings are consigned. In fact, Gaze has noted that texts and images exist along a continuum; asemic texts are situated somewhere at the midpoint, where the distinction between the two types of object is obscured or rendered irrelevant. What this means is that the interpretive stance appropriate to the asemic text is similar or identical to the interpretive stance appropriate to an abstract drawing or painting. It is an interpretive stance rooted in the aesthetic sensibility rather than in semantic inquiry; ultimately, interpretation will be imaginative. For it is only a projection of the interpretive imagination that we can construct the web of correspondences and associations that are capable of filling the asemic text's originary semantic void. It may be helpful to think of this kind of meaning as an emergent property of an asemic composition, which is to say a product or manifestation of the confrontation of the text by the imagination, and not as an independent property in its own right. Simply put, the absence of originary, independent meaning leaves an opening that only the imagination can fill; the imagination will provide its own justification for how it fills that absence, and with what.

From the Asemic to the Polysemic

In confronting a text without an intended, determinate content, interpretation will inevitably be a matter of imaginative flux and metamorphosis—of discovering and rediscovering possible meanings that are always subject to change and motion. This interpretive flux just is a consequence of the way the imagination is. By nature it is plastic and notable for its capacity to generate an almost bewilderingly variety of images and associations through its free play. But it is also a consequence of the text's lack of semantic fixity, itself the logical result of its having no originary meaning, exerting a weak or elastic constraint on imaginative play. What little constraint it does impose—which, as noted above, is a function of its being interpreted aesthetically--is in any case more likely to be enabling rather than prohibiting.

Given the natural flux of imaginative interpretation, any given interpretation of the text's meaning will, in principle, find itself liable to being superseded, subsumed and/or replaced by a subsequent interpretation. The search for an endpoint—a final or even a definitive interpretation—will only be frustrated as new interpretations suggest themselves with each new reading of the text. Any given interpretation will arise as simply one moment within a process whose outcome is always open to change. It is an ongoing process in which anything like a final, unequivocal meaning will always be just out of reach, a process of constant approach and withdrawal, a lateral movement away from the possibility of a fixed message or unequivocal set of references and a movement instead toward some unknown X—a variable the value of which interpretation must constantly determine and re-determine for itself. The apt parallel here is to the paradox of Zeno's Achilles, who can never catch up to the tortoise he's racing. In the same way, interpretation always nears but never quite meets *the* meaning of the asemic text—because there is no such meaning to be met. Interpretation, in a sense, is really chasing itself.

This means, among other things, that no interpretation of an asemic text will be wrong. Asemic writing by definition entails a rejection of the truth claims that follow from, or are at least implicit in, referentiality. The asemic text is neither true nor false but simply is a prompt to the imagination. To the extent that it rejects truth claims and calls instead for an ongoing process of imaginative projection, we might say that asemic writing represents a "weakening" of writing—"weakening" here being used to call up a deliberate echo of "il pensiero debole," or the "weak thought" propounded by philosophers Gianni Vattimo and Pier Aldo Rovatti and others in the 1980s. Weak thought took a perspective that sees our engagement with the world as made up of an ongoing set of interpretations that themselves are based on a history of previous interpretations: experience as interpretation all the way down, in other words, never to arrive at a fixed, unchanging reality transcending all interpretation. Similarly, the asemic text contains no single transcendent meaning to dig down toward and uncover; rather, it is the site of multiple readings and plural meanings that are simply the products of imaginative interpretation.

Thus the asemic text's indeterminacy of meaning and refusal of reference do not equate to asemia per se (if asemia equals the impossibility of meaning) but instead act as the ground of the possibility of meaning—a possibility that realizes itself concretely as multiple meanings in a state of flux. If meaning is possible by virtue of the asemic text's negation of a given, determinate meaning, it is a possibility that manifests itself in the—in principle—open-ended plasticity of the projective imagination. This is writing that pushes beyond writing, writing that pushes interpretation into an endless series of moments or events of an inventive flux—a polysemic, rather than asemic, writing.

Is Silence Golden?

Either No Music, Or a "Return to Principles"

In 1944, "Silence Is Golden," a somewhat curious article by André Breton, appeared in the March-April number of *Modern Music*. What was curious about it was just the fact that an article by Breton should appear in a music journal at all. Breton, the founder and longtime leader of the Surrealist movement who at that moment was enduring war-induced exile in New York, was notorious for his antipathy to music.

There was historical precedent for Breton's attitude. Giorgio de Chirico's 1913 statement "*Point de musique*" ("no music"), in which the painter declared that the visual imagery of painting was a kind of music of its own, may have set the pattern. Similarly Apollinaire, an early mentor of Breton's, had a negative attitude toward music generally and contemporary music specifically, possibly having been influenced in that regard by Alberto Savinio—the musician/painter/writer brother of de Chirico. As for Breton himself, the rejection of music was at least partly explained by the fact that France's emerging interwar avant-garde composers, Les Six, were part of the circle around Jean Cocteau, whom Breton detested: in "Silence Is Golden," Breton quite candidly confesses that his dislike of music is related to his dislike of Cocteau. (This did not prevent one of the six, Georges Auric, from having been a friend of Breton's and from having been briefly mentioned in the latter's first *Manifesto of Surrealism*, although —eventually gravitating toward Cocteau—he never became a part of the Surrealist group.) Other personal reasons may have come into play as well. During the Dada period Breton had spoken well of composer Erik Satie, but the two fell out during the exchanges of vituperation surrounding the collapse of Breton's plans for the Paris Congress of 1922.

Given this background, "Silence Is Golden" seems to represent an offer of détente rather than a continuation of hostilities on Breton's part. It could be, as Breton lets on with elaborate politeness, that it would be bad form to disparage music in a journal dedicated to music —after all, one mustn't insult one's host, no matter what one really thinks of him or her. And the tone of the piece is shot through with ambivalence, which is only reinforced by the entanglements of Breton's prose, the convoluted opacity of which seems to give evidence of an unwillingness to make a statement as explicit as the provocative title would seem to promise. (And the title itself must have struck the reader of *Modern Music*, as it just as easily can strike the reader today, as an arch commentary on Breton's rejection of music—a homely cliché whose appearance in a music journal would unavoidably carry an ironic flourish which, in revealing Breton's actual attitude toward music, rebounds back on itself in the double irony of stating the truth under ironic circumstances. Perhaps.)

Questions of tact having been raised and answered, Breton forthrightly acknowledges the "negative attitude aroused by instrumental music" among the Surrealists and more generally among artists whose medium is language. And he suggests that the musical properties of poetic language are a "compensation" for these artists' rejection of music as such. Nevertheless, he holds out the possibility that the antinomy of poetry and music could be overcome through a "fusion" of verbal musicality and musical composition. Not to suggest how it could be overcome—Breton would give no specifics, modestly acknowledging his "complete ignorance" of compositional methods—but simply that it could be. Despite this diffidence, Breton offers a general program for composers—and it does seem clear that Breton is thinking of composers here and not performers—to pursue.

What Breton called for was a "return to principles" for music, through which hearing could be "reunified." What he seems to have meant by this somewhat puzzling expression was that properly composed music could reconcile the contradiction he saw between perception and imagination: music returned to principles would resolve the opposition between the plain facts of sound picked up by the naked ear and the imaginative constructions through which those facts would be revealed to be the carriers of marvelous or portentous meaning. As with the Hegelian dialectic on which it was based, this reconciliation would take place on a higher plane—on the plane of an overarching super-reality or surreality, properly speaking. Breton's advocacy regarding music is of a piece with the program he set himself from the inception of the Surrealist movement. The reunification of hearing that he called for was just one, medium-specific instance of the larger Surrealist project of reconciling the empirical reality of wakefulness and the imaginative reality of the dream in the higher synthesis of the surreal. And as with poetry and the other arts the Surrealists engaged in, music wouldn't be an end in itself but rather a way of opening up a path to this higher reality—to what Breton in the *Second Manifesto of Surrealism* described as that "certain point of the mind at which life and death, the real and the imagined, past and future, the communicable and the incommunicable, high and low, cease to be perceived as contradictions."

But Music Is Already Disruptive

Breton didn't raise this possibility, specifics of musical composition being, as he admitted, beyond his understanding, but—reading between the lines, and knowing what we know about Surrealist method—could he be suggesting that composers engage in something analogous to the "pure psychic automatism" that, having been used to define Surrealism as early as in the first *Manifesto*, had always been the mainstay of Surrealist creative activity? He doesn't say. But it nevertheless is worth asking: if music is to express an "inner music" comparable to that of poetry, how would it go about doing so? What, in other words, would be the compositional equivalent of automatism —or would there be? (And following Breton's presumed focus on the work of composers, we will only consider composition here rather than performance. Thus the very interesting and valid question of improvised music and its possible relationship to Surrealism and Surrealist automatism must be left for another time.)

It's difficult to see how composition could work on a model derived from automatic writing. As described in the first *Manifesto*, automatism, as the means through which one could record the "actual functioning of thought...in the absence of any control exercised by reason," would require the composer to be reduced to something like the "modest recording instrument" Breton described the automatic writer as having become. Ideally on this model, he or she would be left to transcribe the uncanny associations and incongruous images inhabiting an otherwise submerged or unattended-to psychic reality (which we can think of as the unconscious as, under Freud's influence Breton did, or simply as the unfettered play of the imagination). How to square the strictures of musical notation with the rapid, uncritical movement of the hand essential to automatic writing is by no means obvious.

(I leave out of consideration graphic scores, which could be created through means similar or identical to automatic drawing. But how much fidelity the performance of a graphic score would have to the psychic state that provoked its composition is an open question. It would seem that the degree of interpretation required of the performer would be sufficiently great as to dilute the capacity of the work as played to stand as the direct record of the composer's unconscious impulses. On the other hand it may be that all that's required of this type of compositional automatism is the production of the score, the performance representing an extension of the creative impulse automatism initiated at the moment of the score's coming into being. The parallel here is to what Robert Motherwell termed "plastic automatism"—a method in which a painting or other work of visual art is begun with an automatic gesture which is then elaborated on and completed through the intervention of techniques and formal judgments more or less consciously applied.)

If a way of reconciling the constraints of musical notation with the uncontrolled hand of automatism isn't obvious, then how the associations of the deep imagination could be mapped onto music's peculiar vocabulary and syntax is even less obvious. And that leads to the point—the point of referentiality—where the analogy between poetry and music comes apart.

Beginning with early works like *Les Champs magnétiques* and *Poisson soluble*, Surrealist automatic writing created its effects by disrupting the referential function of language, a function it takes for granted even as it opposes it. Its marvelous images and incongruities are such largely to the extent that they represent a displacement or disorganization of this function. It is from this overturning of the narrative and logical relations ordinarily conveyed by language that automatic writing derives its force. Surrealist automatism steered language away from the conveyance of meaning bound by logic or common sense and pushed it instead toward associative meanings rooted deep in the writer's imagination. Surrealist automatism erased the ordinary semantic content of language, leaving a residue which included the auditory properties of language, or what Breton called the "tonal value of words."

But music is already tonal, both literally and in Breton's more figurative sense, and it has no real capacity to refer to phenomena outside of itself. Lacking this properly semantic or description function, music wouldn't seem to need or to be liable to the kind of signifying rupture Surrealist automatism was meant to bring about. In effect, music is already ruptured. To the extent that it could be said to have extra-formal meaning at all, music already is imaginatively associative.

Interestingly enough, given Breton's official hostility—or at best indifference—toward music, there was at least one attempt at an explicitly Surrealist type of composition undertaken by a composer associated with Surrealism. The composer, André Souris, was a member of the Belgian Surrealist group. Although the Belgian group was allied to Breton's Paris group, it was independent of the Paris group and thus not subject to Breton's dictates. Souris, who was trained in violin, composition and conducting at the Brussels conservatory and who had an interest in the contemporary music of Schoenberg and Stravinsky, joined the Belgian group in 1925 and contributed to a series of musical pamphlets in collaboration with Paul Hooreman, who also was affiliated with Belgian Surrealism.

With Hooreman Souris composed *Trois inventions pour orgue*, a work for barrel organ, a mechanical instrument for street performers somewhat similar to a player piano. The *Trois inventions* was a pastiche of familiar airs taken from popular operettas whose melodies Hooreman and Souris inverted while leaving their rhythms intact. The effect was to scramble the relationships between the notes while maintaining the source material's rhythmic profiles. The inverted melodies would disorient the listeners at the same time that the unmodified rhythms would tease them with hints of the recognizable; the resulting frustration was meant to produce a transformative shock.

What made the *Trois inventions* a specifically Surrealist composition was the extent to which it sought to defamiliarize the familiar and make the banal disruptive—a strategy consistent with the Belgian group's idea of surrealist method, which was to alienate the mundane from its ordinary context, thus turning it into something disconcerting and consequently capable of opening up a rift in experience that would reveal the surreality within the reality of the everyday, common world.

As Souris' music might suggest, perhaps Breton's hypothesizing of a fusion of poetry's inner music and music itself wouldn't necessarily have to be effected through the application of compositional methods analogous to verbal automatism—assuming that such could be devised. Instead, such compositional techniques as collage, disruptive juxtapositions of musical material, distortions of pre-existing or familiar musical sources, or writing focused on timbral or textural effects could offer ways for consciously-working composers to simulate the logic-defying play of the automatic unconscious. Music doesn't have to be written with Surrealist-inspired techniques in order to produce the effects desired by Surrealism; music's real route to the marvelous would seem to lie in its capacity to provoke associations no matter how it was written. Given its nature, the place to look for the inner poetry of music isn't at the point of creation but rather at the point of reception. And here is an irony. In 1928's *Surrealism and Painting,* Breton faulted musical expression—"the most profoundly confusing of all"—for its imprecision and lack of clarity, which he declared to be inferior to the expression afforded by the visual arts. He consequently dismissed music with a much-quoted malediction: "So may night continue to fall upon the orchestra, and may I, who am still seeking something from the world, be left to my silent contemplation, with eyes open or closed, in broad daylight." But it would seem that this imprecision is exactly what makes music suited to the Surrealist project of the reconciliation of the empirical and the imaginative.

It is music's inherent inability to refer with any degree of exactitude that makes it able to provoke associations in a way that more definitely indicative artforms cannot. It is in the nature of instrumental music to be allusive rather than indicative or descriptive—it can't be used to express propositions or precisely describe things or concepts, for example, and this is its advantage. By lacking a specifically referential function, it doesn't foreclose associative or interpretive possibilities but instead opens them up; it suggests in a way analogous to the way an abstract painting suggests. Critic Harold Rosenberg described abstract painting's meaningfulness as inhering in the "emotional reference evoked by color, by shape, by movement;" a similar observation can be made about music, substituting terms like "timbre," "pitch," "phrasing," and "harmony" for Rosenberg's color, shape and movement.

By its very nature, music can hint rather than assert, and Breton's claim in "Silence Is Golden" that music is "independent of the social and moral obligations that limit spoken and written language" would seem to be a concession, if an oblique one, of the liberating effect of music's imprecision of reference. (And it carries a provocative echo of his approving description, in the first *Manifesto*, of automatism as being "exempt from any aesthetic or moral concern.") In its evocative, non-descriptive use of plastic relationships based on sound, music would work in much the same way as the abstract painting, itself influenced by Surrealism, which was beginning to take shape among American painters right around the time "Silence Is Golden" was written.

That Breton understood the ability of sound to unlock creative associations in the listener is clear from his remarks in his article, "The Automatic Message" of 1933. There, he declared that what he called "verbo-auditive automatism" could provoke "the most exalting visual images," images he thought would surpass the images elicited by "verbo-visual" automatism. Clearly, Breton grasped that the sounds of poetry could stimulate an upwelling of images in the reader/listener. (As for the content of the associations precipitated from verbo-auditive automatism...Whether or not they reveal hidden drives and other buried psychological material, or something less dramatic—unreflected-on structures of meaning or elements of temperament, or unsuspected relationships between things half remembered or idly speculated on—is a question best left to others.) By extrapolation—and not one that has very far to go—it's easy to see how music can do the same just as effectively. Music's affinity for the associative imagination may even make it the most surreal of artforms. If one wants to think of it that way.

Surrealism's Musical Afterlife

It isn't surprising, then, that while Breton and other orthodox Surrealists may have rejected music, music did not reject Surrealism. Of composers roughly contemporaneous with Surrealism's first flowering during the interwar period, Edgard Varèse wrote *Arcana* of 1925-1927 having been inspired by dream material, while George Antheil, an American avant-gardist associated with Dada, wrote *La femme: 100 têtes*, a set of piano preludes inspired by Max Ernst's Surrealist collage of that name. Antheil claimed to have been the exception to the Surrealist rule of no music; perhaps for this reason the poet Louis Aragon in 1930 proposed a collaboration in which he and Breton would supply the libretto to an opera whose music was to be written by Antheil. Unsurprisingly, nothing came of it. But since that time, Surrealist poems have been set to music and Surrealist poetry, painting and ideas have inspired instrumental music. Souris continued to compose from a Surrealist aesthetic, even after having been excommunicated from the Belgian Surrealist group in 1936 for having participated in a professional concert in a Dominican church; he would go on to become an important early influence on Pierre Boulez, some of whose own work was inspired by Surrealist poetry. (One could trace a line of descent connecting Surrealism to serialism.)

For Surrealism, silence turned out not to be golden but rather something more akin to pyrite; instead, the gold of time that Breton claimed to seek is as likely to be found through sound as through any other medium. In spite of itself, the movement he founded almost a century ago continues to inspire music even now.

Graphic Scores & Musical Post-Literacy

What decides whether a notational form or system survives is its vitality.
Cornelius Cardew

Notation & Counter Tradition

Toward the end of his comprehensive, multi-volume survey of the history of Western art music, Richard Taruskin raises the possibility that advances in electronic musical technologies have brought us to the cusp of a post-literate age—an age in which the creation, interpretation and preservation of musical compositions depend less and less on standard musical notation. Whether or not musical literacy has gone into eclipse, alternate forms of notation have become increasingly common over the past half-century or so. And while they may not have been designed with the end of standard notation in mind, they do seem to be compatible with, and conducive to, a post-literate musical practice.

Notating a score serves three basic functions: expression of the composer's intention; instruction to allow the performer to realize the composer's intentions; preservation of the work for future realization. In essence, a score is a means of fixing and conveying information about selected properties of sound, to a certain approximation. These properties typically include pitch, duration, dynamics and articulation, as well as the emotion or "feel" a particular passage is meant to have or convey. From the point of view of the tradition of Western art music, representing these properties effectively entails a certain fluency in employing the standard musical notation that has developed since Guido D'Arezzo invented staff notation in the 11th century; interpreting the resulting scores in turn assumes a corresponding fluency in reading standard notation—a musical literacy, in other words. But increasingly, work is being created that doesn't require these skills, hence the suggestion that the current era is a post-literate one.

Renouncing standard notation doesn't necessarily mean renouncing notation; post-literacy doesn't mean illiteracy. At least since the early postwar period there has been a significant counter-tradition of non-standard forms of notation that can fairly be characterized as post-literate in effect if not in original intent. Prominent within this counter-tradition is the graphic score.

Towards a "Creative Ambiguity"

Graphic scores in the modern sense go back to the experiments of the New York School composers of the late 1940s-early 1950s. Earle Brown's *Folio and Four Systems* of 1952-1954 are landmarks in this regard: unconventional scores that bear more of a resemblance to abstract paintings—a very sparse Mondrian comes to mind at times—or lithographs than they do to musical scores.

Brown's scores showed one way to represent sounds, gestures and various parameters of sound—whether defined or undefined—without using conventional symbols for notes, rests, bars and so forth on a five-line stave. To be sure, graphic scores could and did take many forms using many kinds of marks, some of which may take standard notation as a starting point—for example George Crumb's scores written out in circular staves, or Krzysztof Penderecki's use within the staff of symbols representing specific instances of extended string technique. More radical graphic scores, like Brown's, used undefined marks or symbols whose potential open-endedness or outright ambiguity allowed the performer to choose which aspect of the sound or performance they would signify. Perhaps the most striking example of this type of open-endedness is Cornelius Cardew's *Treatise*, an elegant 193-page work that looks rather more like a Robert Motherwell painting than a musical composition.

Paradoxically, Brown's *Folio and Four Systems* as well as other graphic scores from this same period—Morton Feldman's *Projection* series, made on graph paper, or John Cage's *Atlas Eclipticalis*, based on star charts, to choose examples from Brown's fellow New York School composers—were created at a time when avant-garde composers in both Europe and the US were using serial techniques to extend ever more comprehensive control over a composition's various aspects. Graphic scores provided a kind of mirror image of this so-called integral serialism—a methodical inversion, as it were—in their leaving it up to the performer to supply the specific values for a range of musical variables. Brown, a composer with a background as a jazz trumpeter, described his own graphic scores as purporting to furnish a "creatively ambiguous stimulus" that a performer could interpret in any of a number of ways. In a sense the performer would complete the composition by filling in details of pitch, duration, dynamics and so on as hinted at by the score's visual features. But in order to do so effectively, the performer would have to come up with the appropriate interpretive strategy.

Reading Analogically

Cardew described the interpretation of graphic scores as consisting in reading them "intuitively." Intuition may entail many things, but as a strategy for interpreting graphic notation, intuitive interpretation might well rely on the performer's ability or willingness to read marks and signs analogically—to see, e.g., rhythms suggested where marks on the score form regular patterns, or to see the lengths and shapes of lines or forms as indicating durations or the shapes of phrases. (Even to describe phrases as having shapes is to engage in an analogical manner of speaking about musical phenomena; analogical thinking may in fact be inevitable in the conveyance of musical information, graphically scored or not.)

Reading intuitively or analogically is, I would suggest, a post-literate skill or strategy for obtaining (or creating) meaning from a suitably composed text, particularly one embodying a significant degree of indeterminacy. In specifically musical terms such a skill is post-literate because it need not presuppose anything more than a very basic knowledge of the interpretation of conventional scores, if indeed that at all. A rough but suggestive parallel: imagine a written text that conveys information through the shapes and visual patterns of the letters on the page rather than through the ideas communicated by those letters when assembled into words and larger semantic units. Conventional reading skills wouldn't come into play here; rather, other interpretive skills would be called for.

Much information ordinarily carried by a conventional score may be absent from a graphic score—for example, specifics of pitch or duration—and consequently may be in need of the performer's supplying them. In this case the fluent reading, comprehension and precise realization of a composition notated in all of its details naturally wouldn't come into play, as it would with a conventional score. Instead, a more general sense of the composer's intentions will likely provide the major constraint to realization.

These intentions may be set out as verbal instructions prefatory to the main body of the score, or to orally conveyed suggestions. Beyond this, reading the unconventional score requires that at some point the performer enter into it through a radical imaginative leap in order to be able to "hear" what these shapes, lines and other marks might sound like, in the absence of the interpretive constraints imposed by standard conventions.

Given the creative interpretive strategies graphic scores require, it isn't hard to understand the particular appeal these scores hold for experimental musicians. There is something intrinsically "experimental" about the interpretive leap many of them demand—a leap into a notational unknown, where the outcome is potentially unpredictable. But there is an extrinsic reason for the attraction as well. Many experimental musicians were formed outside of traditional musical pedagogy and have come up in musical milieux with strong oral traditions, or those in which, functionally speaking, recordings have taken the place of scores. Nor would fluency in traditional musical notation seem to be especially relevant to experimentalists working with electronics. More generally, a lack of fluency in traditional notation wouldn't be an obstacle to the interpretation of many varieties of graphic notation.

The Varieties of Post-Literate Experience

But by no means are all contemporary graphic scores suited to fully intuitive, largely inventive, post-literate interpretive strategies. Some seem as difficult to realize as the most complex conventional scores and thus as dependent on a foundation in specialized reading skills. Recent scores by Tina Davidson, Michael Maierhof, Takayuki Rai, Keren Rosenbaum, Jack W. Stamps, Kyon Mee Choi and others, for example, take fragmentary elements of standard notation and rearrange them into unexpected configurations or supplement them with verbal instructions and/or unconventional markings to produce visually arresting, provocative scores which still require rigor in reading and in realizing specific authorial intent. If these draw on post-literate interpretation it is by virtue of a post-literacy that presupposes advanced conventional literacy as its starting point.

But others, while still alluding to staves, clefs, articulation and dynamic markings, beams (with and without noteheads) and other symbols drawn from conventional notation, seem to function as did

Brown's early graphic scores, that is, as stimuli for the performer's ingenuity or as enabling constraints on improvisation. Raven Chacon's "pictographic guides" were specifically created in order to help elicit improvised performances from chamber musicians unused to improvisation; Bruce Friedman's O.P.T.I.O.N.S. scores, modular assemblages consisting of symbols often alluding to elements of standard notation, are also meant for structuring improvisations (the acronym stands for Optional Parameters To Improvise Organized Nascent Sounds). Scores by Chris Chalfant, Ivan Vincz and Eoin O'Keeffe take a similar approach. For these scores, as for the elegant graphic designs of John Kannenberg, Joe Pignato, Michael J. Schumacher, Vagn E. Olsson, Hans-Christoph Steiner and Henrik Colding-Jorgensen, one can see in the shapes they contain hints regarding phrase shape, duration and relative pitch, and play accordingly.

Vitality Proves Survival

Finally, to take up the idea stated in the epigraph (and ironically so, given Cardew's later rejection of what he called "graphic music"). Far from being a passing fad of the 1950s and 1960s, experiments with "creatively ambiguous" notation have given rise to a durable and thriving counter-tradition. Graphic scores are again flourishing, or continuing to flourish, because they possess real value for performers and composers alike. While early forms of graphic notation weren't necessarily meant as a way to write for performers not fluent in standard notation, their value as an alternative kind of notation useful for just such performers seems something of a happy, if unintended, consequence. These early graphic scores and their successors could and do quite creatively convey musical information to performers—and composers—who have come up in a world in which traditional musical literacy is no longer a *sine qua non*. We can only expect these scores to become increasingly significant in a post-literate musical world.

Atopia: Soundings from Non-places

If Utopia is an ideal place that doesn't exist—a perfect place that is nowhere except in the imagination—Atopia is a place that does exist, albeit as a non-place. A nowhere that is here.

"Atopia" is a term borrowed from philosopher Franco Rella, who suggested that the modern urban landscape is a kind of place that lacks a sense of specific place—something similar to what Marc Augé has called a "non-place." Atopias are predominantly public places. Or rather public places—certain types of them at any rate—are predominantly atopias.

Certain public spaces—the shopping mall, the interstate highway, the airport terminal and train station, the café, concert hall or cinema, the department store and supermarket— are places whose only interest to us is their use for us. There is no question of inhabiting them; we simply pass through them. They are places to be gotten through and gotten through with; places that generally leave no lasting mark on us after we've done with them. This would seem to be as true of places for entertainment—the amusement parks, movie theaters and the like—as it is of places in which our interest is of a more pragmatic cast. What these disparate kinds of places have in common is that they always present the possibility of use; the atopia, the non-place, is a means *in potentia*. To enter into one is to enter into a dynamic in which the atopia offers itself as an instrumentality or a kind of equipment.

The public place, to the degree that it is an atopia or non-place, is thus for all practical purposes an instrument or utility, something that has meaning in relation to the uses to which it can be put. It is in other words a means toward an end; its function is instrumental. We may not like them, we may find them only tolerable or be indifferent to them, but these atopias are a necessity the way a tool is a necessity given a certain job to be done. A tool to be pushed aside or perhaps handed over to someone else when we've finished with it.

What makes an atopia a non-place is not any lack of physical existence. Nor is its placelessness anything reducible to its physical location or particular architecture—the material facts of the place. Instead, placelessness inheres in the relationships an atopia's material facts have to the people who encounter them and move through them.

Thus place isn't just a location or physically defined area. It's also our way of existing in relation to something. To find one's place; to be in place; to take one's place—in other words, to find where one properly fits in; to assume an assigned function; to be ready to undertake some task given; to take the position that is properly one's own. In all of these meanings the common denominator is the sense of situating oneself, whether in a group or an undertaking. One's place is where one is at home (and we call our home "my place"). Place is something properly ours. Otherwise we are out of place, displaced.

If meaning is the value that attaches to a thing, place, or even another person in relation to a goal or project that thing, place or person offers a means of attaining, then atopias, as instrumental spaces, are nothing if not receptacles of meaning. There is a historical dimension to this in that over time an atopia becomes the site of an accretion of meanings, mostly transient and easily forgotten once their use is done. (And it is this effortless forgetting that gives these non-places a pathos one wouldn't think such anonymous, public places could have.)

The meanings that accrue are our own and those of others to whom we may bear no relation or to whom we are related through a mutual indifference. A kind of non-relation in a non-place.

These non-places show evidence of a history of use, as they play a role in the commitments and projects of people—anonymous people to us here and now—who came before us. Their accrued meanings just are that history of use. We can find in them a complex and highly dynamic—if not to say unstable—interplay of appropriation and alienation. We appropriate the non-place, using it for our purposes and hence having it take on a meaning for us. At the same time this meaning is alienated to the extent that the non-place is just that—a non-place whose transient users are indifferent to the meaning the non-place has for us. Through this interplay of appropriation and alienation the meaning of the public space is constantly being remade. As a built environment, the public space is designated as having a use for us, as having a potential role to play in the uses we and others can make of it whether as facilitating or impeding our activity, or even standing by neutrally.

Our appropriation of the atopia and what it has to offer just is our use of it as a means to attain some goal or realize some project. Through appropriation of the atopia—through grasping it as a set of possibilities that are my possibilities—my own projects and preoccupations are framed and realized (or frustrated). But my use is also alienated to the extent that I use it in the mode of anonymity. From the point of view of the public space or non-place I am not myself as such; I'm just anybody. To the extent that we become—for the moment at any rate—just another user or passer-through, we are refused as concrete individuals and become something like interchangeable ciphers. This kind of alienation is, in a sense, the non-place's price of admission. But the relationship between alienation and appropriation is reciprocal and complex. Much like the experience of being in an atopia.

These atopias are both welcoming and forbidding. As public places for us to occupy and use, they make themselves available to us. At the same time they deny themselves to us by not being ours. It is from this denial that we get the feeling of being out of place or—and this is virtually the same thing—of being in a place that isn't our place. We are in a sense interchangeable with the other people passing through the space; from its point of view there is no difference among us. Consequently, the distinguishing characteristic of the non-place is its neutrality. It takes no sides, as it were, offering itself indiscriminately to any potential user. Public space is in this sense the dwelling place of anonymity; we become anonymous to the extent that we find ourselves within it and for as long as we do. Anonymity just is one way we experience being out of place.

Anonymity in a non-place carries with it the sense of being outside of oneself, of being all surface. When one is out in public, space seems to withdraw around one, leaving one exposed. There is only the look of strangers, with no intervening barriers to block its free play. For that reason, the way we present ourselves in public often takes the form of a hardened surface which acts as a barrier in the absence of physical barriers. The image we project is something like a threshold that isn't meant to be crossed. We may be open to others' looks but we can endeavor to stop them at the surface, at a point of our choosing.

In public space one more often than not is apprehended by strangers as pure presence—as an object more or less inert in its presence, which is to say without reference to its possibilities. One just "is there" as a thing complete in its opacity, without possibilities or potentials to realize, without being in motion toward an aim or desired future state. In other words, not as a finite yet dynamic complex of projects and preoccupations reaching toward an open—because as yet undetermined—future. Instead, the play of the surface, which is all that strangers often really see of us in public, is the play of a mute presence.

(Naturally this brings to mind the Cynics of antiquity. Following Diogenes of Sinope, these itinerant philosophers lived outdoors, making their homes in a condition of homelessness in public spaces. The Cynics inverted the relationship between private and public, negating the private by turning it inside out and making it into something like a public exhibit. The problem of dis-placement doesn't go away so much as it is itself displaced through a kind of proto-performance art involving a reversal of norms.)

In sum, the realm of the atopia or non-place is the realm of anonymity; it is the world as both appropriated and alienated, the world as being there for others to the same extent that it is there for us. It is a place for the play of surfaces, for indifference. We are indifferent to it and it is seemingly indifferent to us—its meanings and equipment are there, as available to us as to anyone else. Nevertheless, these non-places can also provide an opening to an unexpected beauty. Think of Pierre Bezukhov's meeting the Freemason Osip Alexeevich Bazdeev at the Torzhok post station, or the encounter with the extraordinary that the Surrealists hoped to find in the Paris arcades—themselves exemplary non-places. For all its instrumentality, for all its indifference, the atopia may well be the nexus of serendipity; there's no reason something beautiful or moving isn't to be found there. It may only be a matter of looking—or listening.

Imaginary Numbers

A Quasi-Landscape of the Uncanny

A compass would be of no use here; there's no question of getting oriented. Vanishing points seem to proliferate, cross and diverge; lines of sight lose themselves in this strange landscape of cluttered rock. We seem to have been dropped onto an uncomfortable ground of opaque bodies and hard surfaces—a labyrinth that gives us nothing to go on, or a parodic desert of broken buttes and mesas? These forms could be monumental, or they could be minuscule; partly because it is so crowded, the scale of this place is impossible to gauge. As is its origin. Are these naturally occurring piles of rock—glacial deposits, for example—or are they structures artificially, if somewhat sloppily, arranged into heaps? Here as with his other strange paintings of hallucinatory landscapes, Yves Tanguy's *Imaginary Numbers* gives no answers. All we know is that we're here, whatever "here" turns out to be.

Imaginary Numbers was painted in 1954 and may be Tanguy's last work. Like the artist's best-known paintings of dreamlike, ambiguous forms on what appear to be coastal plains or shallow seabeds, *Imaginary Numbers* is a landscape, or quasi-landscape, of the uncanny. Consistent with Tanguy's earlier paintings, *Imaginary Numbers* seems to depict a strange and estranging place best described as *atopos*—alienating and undecidable, a place perpetually out of place with itself. It hints of a nowhere that, although vaguely suggestive of a landscape of rough geology, doesn't seem capable of supporting real existence. To the extent that the world it depicts can only exist in the imagination, it is in line with Tanguy's earlier scenes of biomorphic forms suspended in wide-horizoned spaces. But at this point *Imaginary Numbers* diverges.

What we've come to think of as the typical Tanguy imaginary landscape is a sparsely populated plain—a shoreline or floor under water's edge containing living forms of some sort—perhaps some as yet undiscovered invertebrates or ocean flora. *Imaginary Numbers*' atopic landscape is different. The supple, curvilinear biomorphs of the earlier paintings have been replaced by rigid, hard-edged shapes of geological or quasi-geological origin. If the forms in Tanguy's earlier paintings seem almost weightless, if solid, the forms here are heavy and ground-bound—rounded and cylindrical, suddenly broken off at the top, they resemble petrified stumps or barren rock formations. By the same token, the relatively open spaces of the seabeds and coastal plains of the older paintings have given way to a space stifled with a suffocating density of matter. No bare ground shows through. What isn't covered by rock is apparently surfaced by water; the scene can be read as a network of lakes or canals enclosed by stone walls. Even the color palette has changed. *Imaginary Numbers* is done in an oppressive range of greys, blacks and silver-blues with scattered brown highlights. "Oppressive" in fact is the best way to describe the atmosphere of the atopia the painting depicts, in dramatic contrast to the almost whimsical scenarios of Tanguy's earlier paintings.

Metaphysical Geologies

Like Tanguy's other enigmatic landscapes, *Imaginary Numbers* shows a geography situated as much in the internal world as in its external counterpart. With it, Tanguy charges the visual traces of the physical with the affective valences of his personal metaphysic, a metaphysic fundamentally rooted in dream and recollection. As with so many of those other paintings, *Imaginary Numbers* seems to have emerged from Tanguy's memories of the landscape of coastal Brittany, where he spent summers at the family house in Finistère, the westernmost part of France that juts out into the Atlantic. The marine ambience of the coast permeates Tanguy's paintings of the 1920s and 1930s. That evocation of the open vistas of the shoreline is less true of *Imaginary Numbers* as well as some of the other later paintings Tanguy executed, such as *Multiplication of the Arcs*. But Brittany still seems to be present in these pictures, if through a different complex of allusions. If they no longer contain figures suggestive of marine flora and fauna, the hard-edged, mineral-like images that populate the paintings of the 1940s and 1950s seem to allude to another peculiar feature of Brittany's landscape--the dolmens and menhirs that, dating back to a megalithic culture 6500 years old, are found there. These standing stones would seem to find an echo in the quasi-geological piles of Tanguy's late paintings.

But I want to suggest another possible source for the quasi-geological iconography in Tanguy's later paintings. Some of it, to be sure, may have come from the landscape of the American southwest, which Tanguy saw when visiting his friend Max Ernst in Arizona. But another source may have been the landscape of Tanguy's adopted home. After his move to America in 1939, Tanguy married the American painter Kay Sage and settled in Woodbury, a small town in western Connecticut. Connecticut is full of woods and fields containing old stone walls—more or less loose piles of rocks pulled from ground being plowed for farms, many of which were subsequently abandoned and allowed to revert to forest, leaving the walls behind. These stone walls are frequently encountered throughout the state and are a characteristic part of the background texture of the physical environment. It's possible that these local standing stones, which might strike a Breton as miniature parodies of menhirs, came to Tanguy's conscious or unconscious notice and from there made their way into paintings executed in America.

Perhaps coincidentally, *Imaginary Numbers* contains another suggestive allusion to the landscape of Tanguy's adopted state. The upthrusting, abruptly truncated formations in the painting recall the bare, columnar faces of the basalt traprock ridges that run on a north-south axis through central Connecticut from Long Island Sound and reach all the way up to Vermont. In addition, the heaps of broken rock on the ridges' talus slopes resemble the clutter of figures in Tanguy's canvas. But although the Connecticut traprock ridges and the figures in *Imaginary Numbers* show a striking similarity of shape and disposition, they do have one significant difference: color. Because of their high iron content the traprock ridges feature the distinctive, reddish tinge of oxidation. Tanguy's painting, as already noted, is composed of greys, blacks, and silver-blues—colors drawn from the opposite end of the scale.

We don't know if Tanguy was familiar with Connecticut's concatenation of traprock ridges. Still, it's an intriguing possibility that *Imaginary Numbers* represents an oneiric hybrid of the geologies of the Old and New Worlds—of Tanguy's childhood and adult environments—fused from that Surrealist vantage point where contradictions and incongruities dissolve. By extension, we might want to see the painting's coincidence of forms as an example of what the Surrealists characterized as objective chance—a convergence of unlikely events or objects that carries a profound, if not immediately apparent, significance for the person touched by it. A metaphysical significance, in the sense that what is revealed is some occult truth about the reality beneath the appearance, a reality animated by affective need and expectation, and perhaps a variety of self-knowledge ordinarily unnoticed or ignored.

If what we're seeing in *Imaginary Numbers* is a representation of a landscape or landscapes Tanguy knew, it isn't a literal representation of the physical places' features so much as a metaphysical image, one screened through the distorting lenses of dream, affect, and the variably reliable faculty of memory. Through this process of transformation perception passes from the purely empirical to the affectively meaningful and the imaginatively resonant; committed to canvas it discloses a set of complex and contraposed affective meanings entangling the recollection of roots with the atopia of uprootedness. It is in the context of these contradictory moods that the disorientation and out-of-placeness—the sense of being *atopos*—that Tanguy's claustrophobic, estranging landscape hints at truly come into their own. Tanguy's painting doesn't give direct, unambiguous evidence of the visible places provoking this meaning but rather is rooted in a lived situation whose landmarks are the products of emotional attraction and repulsion, of need and desire, rather than of geology and erosion.

Imaginary Numbers as Poetic Analogy

Like Tanguy's imaginary landscape, the mathematical objects known as imaginary numbers are *atopos*—strange and apparently not to be encountered in any actually existing world. Their strangeness consists in their seemingly self-contradictory nature: they involve the square root of a negative number, contradicting the mathematical truth that any number times itself produces a positive number, even if the multiplied number is negative. Given this contradiction, square roots of negative numbers shouldn't exist—they should be purely imaginary, as Descartes, who gave them that name, thought—but they do in fact exist and are used for electrical engineering, probability calculations and communications applications.

In giving their name to Tanguy's painting, imaginary numbers serve as a metaphor for the reality of what otherwise would be dismissed as "merely" imaginary. In an odd way they symbolize the ultimate point Surrealism aimed at: the point at which the contradictions between dream and waking reality, consciousness and unconsciousness, and perception and imagination, would dissolve. It is a point Tanguy's imaginary landscapes, with their metaphysical overtones, approach. To the extent that *Imaginary Numbers* depicts a geology with metaphysical overtones, it stands as the image of a reality transposed to and revealed by the affective realms of dream and memory—an image that, in the best traditions of Surrealism, appears to refuse the constraints of the real, but only for as long as the latter is understood to be coterminous with the plain, unmetaphysical world of mute things and meaningless events. But like imaginary numbers, whose reason for being initially seemed to consist in their impossibility of being, Tanguy's imaginary geology doesn't refuse reality—or better, is not refused by reality—so much as it represents a reality permeated by the super reality of human purpose as manifested through the filter of affective meaning. Like imaginary numbers, Tanguy's imaginary rockscape turns out to have a real existence and to that degree, its title serves as what André Breton, in his essay "Ascendant Sign," defined as a poetic analogy: a means of comprehending one thing through another by virtue of a relationship between two objects of thought from different planes that, through a kind of non-logical apprehension, reveal themselves to be somehow interdependent. Taken as a poetic analogy, imaginary numbers demonstrate the interdependence of the imagination and reality—or put in other terms, of the physical and metaphysical—an interdependence the recognition of which allows the portending coincidences of objective chance to be recognized and deciphered.

Anxiety & Anticipation

As Michel Carrouges points out in his study of the basic concepts of Surrealism, objective chance has a "dark zone" disclosed as a presentiment that may make itself known through feelings of panic, anxiety and estrangement. This dark zone derives from the way objective chance appears to upset the uniquely human mode of temporality—the projection forward into a future that may or may not be. Rather than presenting a future of possibility (and the possibility of failure), objective chance as the occasion of presentiment appears instead to be revelatory of destiny; read that way, the coincidences it consists in seem to point uncannily toward an already accomplished future, which it hints at through its disquieting intimations of what (apparently) necessarily must be. Such a reading would be too superficial, however, and deeply misleading. The destiny objective chance reveals isn't something preordained and always already accomplished but instead is a conditional destiny, one contingent on the person to whom it attaches. To a reasonable approximation it is the kind of destiny that Heraclitus, as he's often been translated as saying, framed in terms of one's fate (*daimon*) consisting in one's character (*ethos*)—a destiny in the form of a likelihood dependent on one's own pattern of actions, desires, limitations and self-knowledge (or ignorance) that requires the right convergence of events for its realization.

If objective chance is a function of the existential structures unique to a given person, then, as Surrealism would seem to have had it, it could be expected to disclose itself through that person's unconscious (however defined) by way of automatic writing or visual imagery. These latter media would provide what Ferdinand Alquié, in *The Philosophy of Surrealism*, described as "poetic flashes [that] come to enrich human experience in the manner of premonitions" (p. 97). Just such premonitory flashes would appear to be embodied in *Imaginary Numbers*, whose atopic atmosphere may derive from something over and above its apparent allusions to dream and memory. It may derive instead from the anxiety that often accompanies anticipation.

Anticipation, in the form of a sign of a coming event, can be read in the sky above *Imaginary Numbers*' rockscape. It is thick with bilious black clouds gathered in rolls, the kind of sky that precedes a storm or tornado. In light of the fact that the painting, completed shortly before Tanguy died suddenly of a cerebral hemorrhage in January, 1955, was probably his last, the sky reads less like the neutral depiction of certain meteorological conditions than as an omen. Not only does the sky seem a sign of impending death, but the truncated cylindrical shapes of the rock formations bear an uncanny resemblance to broken columns—a form of funeral architecture used to memorialize someone dying suddenly or in the prime of life. (Interestingly enough, in his 1927 painting *Death Watching His Family*, Tanguy included as a central image a short, stout, apparently stone cylindrical form that appears to be a broken column.) When read this way, *Imaginary Numbers* begins to resemble the cloud-overshadowed landscape of a cluttered urban cemetery.

If dream and memory present the empirical facts of experience through the filters of affect and need (or desire), anticipation projects affect and desire forward onto facts of experience that have yet to be, if they are to be at all. It is through such anticipation, Surrealism held, that objective chance would allow itself to be perceived. But in the end, what anticipation opens up to, and what objective chance can be said to reveal, beyond the specific events that may appear destined for any given individual, is the ultimate nothingness of fate—the abyss over which human existence is constructed. There is thus an irreducibly tragic dimension to objective chance, no matter how marvelous its outward manifestation. With its claustrophobia-inducing labyrinths dead-ending, metaphysically speaking, at this zero point of nothingness—a point where dream, memory and premonition converge—*Imaginary Numbers* follows objective chance to its ultimate conclusion.

The Silver Age of Surrealism in Exile

Toward the end of his wartime exile in America, André Breton traveled to the Gaspe Peninsula in Quebec. There, between August and November, 1944, he wrote *Arcane 17*, one of the late masterpieces of Surrealism. *Arcane 17* is a strange book that's lost little of its strangeness over time. Not quite an essay or prose poem, it is instead a rich text of reflections and outcry, a meditation on war and loss woven together by allusions to myth and myth-inspired exegesis. The title refers to the seventeenth card in the tarot deck's trump suit: The Star. Breton's elaboration of the supposed occult meaning of the card forms one of the major leitmotifs running throughout the work, along with his invocation of the myth of Melusine, a creature half woman and half fish that rhymes, metaphorically, with The Star's image of a woman pouring water into a river. The book was written by the water, in view of the famous Roche Percé; its themes are framed by water: by water as an image of mythical import. In a way, *Arcane 17* represents the culmination of a process that had been taking place within Surrealism since it crossed the Atlantic: the turn toward myth as a major source of inspiration and correlatively, a new understanding of automatism and its role in the creation of artworks.

Although Breton's period in exile was by all accounts an unhappy one, it was, ironically, also a period that could fairly be described as Surrealism's Silver Age. If the heroic early years between the two world wars was Surrealism's Golden Age—a time of discovery and daring—the 1940s and American exile saw on the one hand the maturation and solidifying of the conceptual edifice of Surrealism and on the other, an infusion of new energy obtained from a new generation of artists.

Both of these forces were decisive for the flourishing Surrealism would experience during what otherwise could have been years in the wilderness. From its engagement with the symbolic world of myth, Surrealism acquired an altered perspective on its self-understanding along with an expanded vocabulary of concepts and images; this ancient source lent it a degree of rejuvenation as well as maturity. From the younger American artists it attracted, Surrealism obtained new techniques and processes for creating artworks, techniques and processes that would bring an altered understanding of the role of automatism within Surrealist art. But these forces, which together pushed Surrealism into its Silver Age, would also prove to be centrifugal.

The Surrealist Turn to Myth and The Great Transparents

To be sure, Breton's interest in myth during the 1940s wasn't unprecedented. From the beginning there had always been a fascination among the Surrealists with non-Western cultures, particularly those of Oceania and the aboriginal inhabitants of North America; the first Surrealist journals contained articles on topics in anthropology, ethnology and archaeology in addition to literary writing. If during this early period myth hadn't yet taken on an important or even central role in Surrealism's self-consciousness, the way certainly was being prepared for it to do so. By 1937, in his important theoretical text "Nonnational Boundaries of Surrealism," Breton explicitly appealed to "the eternal lure of myths and symbols" as providing the sole outlet for the "innermost emotion of a human being" (p. 13). Breton thought that it would be through the abeyance of rational control that these emotions would be released. The affinity between Surrealism and myth here is quite clear: the core Surrealist practice of automatism in all of its forms—written, oral, or visual imagery—entailed the suspension of reason's critical functions and, presumably bringing to the surface ordinarily submerged deep emotions and desires, could be expected to express itself in a vocabulary drawn from myth.

And certainly by 1942, Surrealism had taken an explicitly mythical turn. For the *First Papers of Surrealism* exhibition in October-November of that year, Breton called for Surrealism to "rejoin the most durable traditions" of humankind (Tashjian, p. 232). A year later, in a combined second and third number the New York-based Surrealist review *VVV* ran a piece with the provocative title, "Concerning the Present-Day Relative Attractions of Various Creatures in Mythology and Legend." Twenty-one Surrealists and others—these latter including Lionel Abel and Harold Rosenberg—were asked to rank fifteen mythical or fantastic figures in order of their "contemporary relative attraction." (For those curious, the top three were, in order, Sphinx, Chimera and Minotaur.)

It was also in 1942 that Surrealism saw one of its odder episodes when Breton announced the creation of a new myth. Such a move wasn't entirely surprising; in "Nonnational Boundaries of Surrealism" Breton declared that the "self-allotted task" of Surrealism was to elaborate a "collective myth" appropriate to its time (pp. 14-15). Thus it was that in the final section of his "Prolegomena to a Third Manifesto of Surrealism or Not," published in June, 1942 in the first issue of *VVV*, Breton introduced his myth in the form of *Les Grands Transparents*. Breton's Great Transparents were "hypothetical beings" of immense scale and strangeness, compared to whom humans would appear as insignificant specks. The nature and existence of these beings, Breton suggests, might possibly be inferred from vast natural and human upheavals—he names cyclones and wars as two such—and may "mysteriously reveal themselves to us when we are afraid and when we are conscious of the workings of chance." (This last point is particularly notable in that it seems to connect the new Surrealist myth of the Great Transparents with the old Surrealist myth of objective chance.)

As with many of Breton's declarations this one is hedged with qualifications and couched in the language of counterfactuals and conditional auxiliary verbs, but what nevertheless comes through

Breton's habitual indirection is an almost palpable desire to believe in these imagined, if not imaginary, beings: they may "result from a mirage" but at the same time, should they not be "given a chance to show themselves?"

Although Breton cites Novalis, William James and Emile Duclaux as his sources or inspiration for the Great Transparents, it appears that he got the idea from Chilean-born painterMatta just before the outbreak of war, when the latter was in Paris (Sawin, p. 199; Tashjian, p. 211). For his part, Matta appears to have gotten the idea from P.D. Ouspensky's *Tertium Organum*, a book whose treatment of four-dimensional geometry exerted a significant influence on the painter's developing aesthetic and metaphysic. Figures like the Great Transparents turn up in his paintings of the late 1930s and early 1940s; the floating forms in *Prescience*, for instance, appear to be transparent beings whose transparency may be an allusion to their four-dimensionality (since the four-dimensional perspective would reveal the interior and exterior of a figure simultaneously). Significantly, in *Tertium Organum* Ouspensky quotes the mathematician Charles Howard Hinton's suggestion, from the latter's 1888 book *A New Era of Thought*, that there are four-dimensional "high intelligences by whom we are surrounded; we feel them but do not realize them" (Ouspensky, p. 207). It seems likely that Breton's Great Transparents represent a transposition into a deliberately mythological key of Hinton's invisible "high intelligences."

Breton was certainly aware of Matta's enthusiasm for the fourth dimension. In his 1939 essay "The Most Recent Tendencies in Surrealist Painting," Breton remarks on the interest among younger painters in seeing beyond the three-dimensional world and creating the "suggestive representation" of a four-dimensional world. In this connection he explicitly names Matta and the latter's attempts to depict four-dimensional space through the use of multiple horizons (*Surrealism and Painting*, pp. 148-149).

Obligingly enough, some of the Surrealist and Surrealist-associated painters began to create works on the theme of the Great Transparents. Kurt Seligmann painted *Melusine and the Great Transparents*; Gerome Kamrowski did a picture with the cinematic title *Script for an Impossible Documentary: The Great Invisibles*; and Matta in the early 1940s was putting transparent figures he called "vitreuers" (roughly, "glassy ones") in his paintings of four-dimensional spaces (Sawin, p. 217). The Great Transparents also showed up in the catalogue to the *First Papers of Surrealism* show, appearing in a section Breton put together and titled "On the Survival of Certain Myths and on Some Other Myths in Growth and Formation." There, Breton collected some images and texts on mythic or occult themes, ending with The Great Transparents, illustrated with a manipulated photograph by David Hare.

Although the Great Transparents did not become the new social myth Breton had hoped they would—in Kamrowski's well-known remark, they were a "myth that didn't fly" (Sawin, p. 217)—espousing them at least was a public demonstration of Breton's seriousness in engaging the question of the need for myth in modern times. And it seems the Great Transparents didn't fade away entirely; in a curious reprise they are obliquely alluded to in Breton's repeating, in a 1963 essay on painter Enrico Baj, the suggestion that humans may be to greater creatures what lice are to humans: "irritants on the skin of far larger animals quite outside our scale of references" (*Surrealism and Painting*, p. 399).

Influences from the Periphery

To some extent, Breton's thinking about the role of myth in Surrealism was formulated in dialogue with Wolfgang Paalen's counter-thinking. Although lesser-known today than many of the other artists associated with Surrealism, Paalen in the late 1930s-early 1940s played a pivotal role in developing Surrealist and Surrealist-inspired visual arts on both the theoretical and practical levels. An

Austrian by birth, Paalen had settled in Mexico in late 1939 after leaving Paris in May for the North American Pacific Northwest, where he studied native cultures. While in Paris in the mid-1930s he had met Breton and began associating with the Surrealist group. His invention of fumage—a method of creating images by using the smoke and ash of a burning candle to produce visual patterns on a canvas or other surface—was one of his contributions to the technical innovations that were then being introduced into Surrealist art-making. If, arguably, for Surrealism in exile Mexico represented the periphery to New York's center, Paalen's contributions to Surrealism's Silver Age ferment were anything but peripheral.

Beyond his influence on the extension of Surrealism's technical resources, it was Paalen's interest in totemism, already evident in his series of *Totemic Landscape* paintings of 1937, that would have an impact on Surrealism, particularly in regard to its mythic turn. In fact, it was this interest that had led him to the Pacific Northwest and ultimately to Mexico. His anthropological research there helped him to formulate an understanding of myth and its role in recovering a hypothesized primordial past; he drew on this understanding when articulating his aesthetic theories in *DYN*, the journal he published between 1942 and 1944 in Mexico. For example, in his editorial preface to the special Amerindian double number, published in December, 1943, Paalen, in what amounts to a programmatic statement, declared that art could "reunite us with our prehistoric past and thus…enable us to grasp the memories of unfathomable ages." He further called for a "universal art" that would help shape a new "world-consciousness." In "Totem Art," from the same issue, Paalen held up the sculpture of the Pacific Northwest Coast natives as exemplary of an art that was created for the emblematic realization of a communal or collective experience of life and not simply for personal consumption. (Rushing, p. 275). Paalen was striving for a similar goal of primordial, collective universality with his own art, and felt that the values embodied in totemic art could somehow be translated into contemporary art.

It was in the first number of *DYN* that he declared his "Farewell to Surrealism," setting the stage for him to play an independent role in influencing the younger generation of Surrealist-allied artists, among them Matta and most importantly, the American Robert Motherwell, both of whom spent time in Mexico with Paalen. Motherwell in particular played an important role in bringing Paalen's ideas back to New York. Thus it is possible to see Paalen as a challenger to Breton for intellectual leadership of the artists interested in myth and the unconscious, and to an extent he was; at the same time, it's also possible to see Paalen and Breton as engaged in a surreptitious dialogue of mutual interest and mutual influence during the war years. Their disagreements may at the time have seemed significant, but on the crucial matter of the role of myth in modern life, they now appear to have been in basic agreement. Opposition there may have been, but intellectual stimulation was its ultimate effect.

For both Paalen and Breton, myth offered a still-indispensable way of orienting oneself in the world, an interpretive stance belonging to a fundamental stratum of the human psyche. Thus for both, myth was a largely psychological phenomenon. But it's possible to see their engagement of myth as carrying an existential implication going beyond psychology. The mythic stance is an existential one precisely to the degree that it confronts the world as a set of given meaningful possibilities in relation to which one must act. What gives it a peculiarly mythical force is its recognition of the marvelous or the extraordinary as being among these possibilities.

More than that, the mythic stance sees possibility itself as being underwritten by the extraordinary: in its permeation of the world as such, the marvelous is the *sine qua non* of the mundane; it is the touchstone in relation to which meaning arises as meaning. It only remains for the marvelous to be disclosed as the ground of meaning. In sum, the interpretive stance encoded in myth is, from the existential point of view, a way of finding one's bearings and grasping the world as a meaningful environment latent with signs and associations that, in revealing the extraordinary in the ordinary, speak directly or indirectly to the perennial human predicament.

Toward a New Automatism, and a New Art

At about the same time that Paalen's and Breton's positions were converging on myth, the path the younger painters were exploring diverged from Surrealism. Surrealist art had already undergone a transformation; what is striking about Surrealist painting during the early 1940s is its shift from an earlier aesthetic that often relied on the juxtaposition of unrelated objects—a kind of visual realization of objective chance or of Lautréamont's encounter of an umbrella and a sewing machine on an operating table—to a portrayal of ambiguous spaces and strange life forms. Surrealist art was in transition, both stylistically and methodologically. One of these transitions concerned the conception of psychic automatism, the role and function of which would be substantially altered during Surrealism's American exile.

Psychic automatism was, from the beginning, one of the fundamental principles of Surrealism. In the first *Manifesto of Surrealism*, Breton defined Surrealism simply as "pure psychic automatism." For the original Surrealists this meant, in practical terms, the unconstrained disclosure of the unconscious through automatic writing or other methods using language as a medium. As Surrealist activity expanded into the visual arts, the question of transposing psychic automatism from a linguistic to a plastic medium arose. It was a question with two parts: what would a visualized unconscious look like, and how—by what method—could it be conveyed?

The solutions to the problem of transposition were multiple, varying from, at one extreme, Dali's transcriptions of dream images in an academic style, and at the other extreme, Masson's automatic drawings of the early 1920s. Masson left the Surrealist movement in 1929 and abandoned automatic methods for consciously-controlled imagery, but shortly after reconciling with Breton in 1937 he had once again begun to practice visual automatism with a method that explicitly renounced the constraints of conscious control. As he described the process in "Painting as a Wager": "Seize your inspiration in that state of ecstasy and paroxysm in which mind and body coincide and regain their lost unity. Let execution be a lightning-swift and automatic act" (Sawin, p. 175). In theory, at least, this comes close to a programmatic statement for a psychic automatism at its purest; it testifies to a renewed interest in returning to Surrealism's first principles. Thus by 1941, Breton could assert, with a marked tone of triumphalism, that the "very latest examples of surrealist painting…show a marked return to *automatism*…we have had to wait until fifteen years after the *Surrealist Manifesto* called for it to be put into practice enthusiastically for *absolute* automatism to make its appearance on the level of plastic creation" (Breton, *Surrealism and Painting*, p. 145). This return to automatism didn't represent a simple recapitulation of old methods but instead had been facilitated by the recent development of new techniques, among them decalcomania, frottage, and fumage.

Also among the new automatist techniques developed during the late 1930s-early 1940s was a kind of proto-gestural painting introduced by Matta. Matta had trained as an architect and was a self-taught painter; perhaps for this reason he felt freer to explore unorthodox methods than would someone with a more conventional background. During a visit to Gordon Onslow-Ford in Switzerland, Matta experimented with applying paint directly to the canvas with a palette knife and then spreading it around rapidly with his fingers (Onslow-Ford). In the Surrealist review *Minotaure* in 1939, Breton described Matta's direct application of paint as "divination through color"; certainly, it was a way for Matta to achieve his project of creating a psychic automatism that could depict what he called "*morphologie psychologique*"—psychological morphology, or the ongoing transformations of the psyche. By his definition, automatism was "a method of reading 'live' the actual function of thinking at the same speed as the matter we are thinking of, to read at the speed of events, to grasp unconscious material functioning in our memory with the tools at our disposal. Automatism means that the irrational and the rational are running parallel and can send sparks into each other and light the common road" (Hobbs, p. 59).

Matta's psychological morphology was as much a challenge to the orthodox Surrealist group as it was a breakthrough for his own aesthetic. After moving to New York in November, 1939, Matta made contact with some of the younger American painters there. According to Motherwell's recollection, Matta intended to carry Surrealist theory further than had the orthodox Surrealists, with whom he had what Motherwell described as a "love-hate relationship" (Shapiro and Shapiro, pp. 37-38). To that end, Matta around 1942 gathered about him a small circle that included, in addition to Motherwell, William Baziotes, Jackson Pollock, Gerome Kamrowski and Peter Busa, and planned a show at Peggy Guggenheim's gallery that would serve notice to the older Surrealists that they'd been outdone by the younger, less compromising artists. The show never took place—Matta apparently lost interest or had second thoughts about potentially provoking a break with Breton—but his longer-term influence on the American painters would prove to be profound.

While Matta was revivifying automatism in New York, Paalen was himself laying the intellectual foundations of a rethinking of automatism and its place in the expressive economy of painting. It was in this regard that Paalen was particularly influential on the new generation of artists; the path he laid out in addressing the Surrealist problem of what psychic automatism could mean, and how it could be effectively implemented in the visual arts was, like Matta's brief alliance with the younger New York painters, to have a lasting effect on the development of postwar painting.

Paalen set out his basic principles in the essay "The New Image," written in summer, 1941 and published in *DYN*'s inaugural number in April/May, 1942. Paalen's essential point was that the "relevant aspects of automatism" were to be found in "techniques of *divination*, whose function is to sense unexpected images in aesthetically amorphous material" (Paalen, p. 41). Automatism would be a mode of seeing if not of seership, a way of diving form in the originally formless material it made its object. Paalen further described it as "incantatory technique" rather than a mode of "creative expression" (Paalen, p. 41); it was, in other words, a means of setting out rather than a point of arrival. Although not simply a vehicle of expression, neither was the new image a means of replicating or interpreting external reality; rather, the "true raw material" of the new automatism would consist in the "kaleidoscopic flow" of the painter's inner world (Paalen, p. 42). Above all, the new image would not represent but instead would prefigure or project "potentialities of existence" (Paalen, p. 53).

The critical point of this kind of automatism is that cessation of conscious control only represented the first stage; after that, choice once again asserted itself, and the material of the work once again became the site of possibilities to be realized according to the specific project the artist brought to it. Automatism thus conceived involved the meeting of chance and project, of accident and intention. This represented a significant break with Surrealist orthodoxy in that it marked a turn from the "pure psychic automatism" of the original surrealism to what Motherwell called "plastic automatism." Plastic automatism recognized the enabling constraint of the material medium in forming the painting, and while many of the younger painters, particularly those under the influence of Jung, considered the subject matter of their paintings to consist in the signification of universal, and at least quasi-mythical inner patterns of experience, their automatism was *plastic* precisely to the extent that it recognized the constructive role that formal and material elements had in the creation of that content. Their automatism implied, in effect, the ascendency of matter over myth. If the unconscious showed itself it was in the initial, free gesture; as Peter Busa put it when describing the automatist sessions with Matta, "one didn't have an image to begin with, but rather a hand and a motor ability" (Sawin, p. 241). The image emerged from the meeting of imagination and material, through the hand. And, in perhaps the most significant deviation from Surrealist orthodoxy, for the American painters it no longer bore the trace of the marvelous. In Motherwell's formulation, Paalen's divination becomes refigured as the mind "realizing itself in color and space" through the medium of the painting, whose content is rooted in "the interplay of a sentient being and the external world" (Motherwell, p. 32). This notion of mind disclosing itself through the plastic values of the medium is recognizable in the intellectual substrate of the Abstract Expressionist painting that became the dominant mode of American visual art after the war.

Thus despite the hyperbole to which he was prone, Breton in praising "The Most Recent Tendencies in Surrealist Painting" did describe a real phenomenon of long-term significance to painting: the adoption by many younger painters of new methods for realizing an art derived from psychic automatism. The irony is that some of these painters, joined later by those they met in America, adopted automatist methods with ends in mind that would differ significantly from those of Breton and orthodox Surrealism. But like a Cadmus of the marvelous, Breton and the ideas he had helped to inspire—some in agreement, some in opposition—would turn out to be so many dragon's teeth from which that new generation of painting could spring.

The American turn to automatism would become, in effect, a turn away from Surrealism and its visions of the marvelous and instead would represent a reorientation toward what would eventually be an independent school of abstract painting. It would be the turn from psychic automatism *per se* to Motherwell's "plastic automatism" and through it, to the gestural painting of the New York School. Surrealism's American exile, although notable for its energetic embrace of new ideas and new artistic techniques was, in the end, a period of transition, not only for the older European Surrealists, but for the younger American artists they helped inspire and who would eclipse them in the postwar era. Out of the Silver Age of Surrealism was born what arguably would be a Golden Age of American painting.

Free Improvisation as Experience & Self-Disclosure

In his 1952 essay *The American Action Painters,* Harold Rosenberg set the template for a particular understanding of the abstract painting of the day. It was an understanding based on a mythology—mythology in the sense of a primal story that makes sense of something without having to be literally true. This was the myth of painting as spontaneous gesture, the product of which—the painting itself--was the record of an event. This event consisted in the existential encounter of the painter, acting freely and without any premeditated notion of what would result, with the blank canvas. As Rosenberg memorably put it, the empty picture plane became "an arena in which to act," the site of a process rather than a place on which to paint a picture. Call it painting understood as performance. Like many clichés, this one became established because it did contain a core of truth.

Rosenberg's essay drew on ideas taken from the Existentialism that was in vogue in the immediate postwar period and that—partly through his influence as a critic—permeated talk about art at the time. To the extent that the painters Rosenberg described were acting spontaneously—and certainly not all of them were—his speculation did capture something of what was in fact happening with them, both in terms of what they experienced while painting and what kind of relationship there was between their artistic processes and products. Although art is rarely spoken about in these terms any longer, a view of artistic activity as rooted in the realization of the artist's free, concrete choices does still seem relevant to understanding how certain kinds of art are made. It particularly seems to describe what many of us experience in the practice of free improvisation in music and sound art. But a more complete picture would have to look beyond the notion of free choice and see it as being afforded by an often unarticulated background of technical skill and intuitions about form. In short, the experience of free improvisation is the experience of freedom, but it is a freedom structured by a rich background of practical knowledge expressed in gestures holistically fusing intention and action.

The Experience of Free Improvisation

In the moment of playing a free improvisation, we do seem to act on the basis of unconstrained choices. Any given gesture—meaning here a physical action producing an intended sound--may be made with reference to what came before it, but it doesn't feel determined by that precedent. I can for example choose to play a sequence of notes or unpitched sounds that would fit in some way with what was just played, or I can choose to play something that would break with it entirely. The improvisation may seem to be unfolding in a particular way, but I can always choose to play otherwise and thus to redirect it, to convert its mood and developing formal structures into something quite other than what it was.

In part, the experience of free improvisation is the experience of freedom because there is no pre-given formal structure or work to which our individual choices must conform. Instead, the freely improvised performance is directed toward an open possibility—a possibility made open by the lack of a preexisting composition to be realized in and by the performance. Free improvisation is in this sense the exploration of a country that doesn't exist until it's conjured into being by that very same exploration.

In practical terms, this means that the object of the gesture—the sound, phrase or, seen from a more encompassing perspective, the entire performance—doesn't exist prior to the gesture and only comes into being with the gesture itself. As a result, the decisions we make while playing from moment-to-moment are decisions that transcend these moments toward some as yet unattained formal/plastic state of affairs in which sounds find their places within, against and among each other. It is only from these individual decisions that a musical object comes into being; its formal qualities and structures are the audible results of the individual choices that informed and produced our musical gestures. The completely improvised musical object, in other words, just is the sum of the individual actions—gestures chosen freely against a background of possibilities—that go into its making. It is constituted by the choices made in real time that are themselves aimed at the external, open field of possibility that is the object's not having existed yet.

Seen this way, free improvisation is free to the extent that it consists in making a choice of form in the absence of controlling formal constraints. If the sonic plasticity of the object—which is to say the formal qualities of the freely improvised performance—is not given in advance, there is at any given time no a priori, external reason why I should play notes chosen from, say, scale X rather than from mode Y, or a particular rhythmic figure or vertical conjunction of sounds rather than another, and so forth. All of these choices are mine to make in the moment; I am free to shape the performance as it unfolds in real time according to these choices and to modify and convert them as seems appropriate at any given moment.

Freedom & Skill

And yet this picture of freedom needs to be qualified in important ways. If we can speak of free improvisation as lacking the external constraints imposed by pre-given forms, things become quite different when we consider the role of internal constraints. Here the freedom of the free improviser becomes conditioned freedom. Once we step back and look beyond the moment we can see that what appears at first to be a completely free choice isn't entirely free. As improvisers we don't start from nothing; we instead act in a way that's always already constituted by our store of practical knowledge. We do choose, but within certain limits intimately connected to our personal histories and facilities as artists. These limits include such things as our technical skills and the consequent repertoire of things we know how to do, our expectations of what an improvised work should sound like, our ability to listen and respond in an interesting and appropriate way, and so on. This practical knowledge is a function of our competence as improvising musicians, all told, as well as of the intuitive sense of form we bring to any improvisational situation.

It is this competence or skill that is the practical ground underlying and facilitating the feeling of freedom in performance. Our ability to play improvised music appropriately is the result of those internalized, intuitively available musical patterns that come with learning and practice—what we mean when we say that we "have something under our fingers"—and that we can turn to in the moment. This kind of internalized skill allows us to immerse ourselves in the moment-to-moment unfolding of the improvisation without the need to reflect on what we are doing or how we are doing it. We just know how to do it, within the limits of our practical ability.

In addition to the requisite instrumental and listening skills, the free improviser has an intuitive—that is to say a pre-deliberative—sense of the formal relationships that structure a performance. This intuitive sense of form includes such elements as our sense of the rhythmic and pitch balance of a phrase; the contrasting or complementary relationships among pitches, timbres and rhythms; the degree of density and dynamics desirable at any given moment in the performance; the placement of sounds and silences as constituent parts of an overall musical structure, and the like. All of this constitutes the background of expectations against which our individual choices take place and which is available as a kind of reservoir of possibilities to be realized in any given musical gesture or set of gestures.

The upshot of all this is that the improvised musical gesture isn't a blind act arising in a vacuum but instead is grounded in the improviser's training and experiences as an improviser. In practical terms, this means that it embodies—quite literally—an intuitive sense of phrase structure and balance, duration, timbre and pitch, as well as such ensemble features as harmony and counterpoint and is made possible by the technical means we possess to produce it. Improvisation as a gesture with materials—to borrow Rosenberg's phrase—thus takes place within a context of certain given conditions that, taken together, function as a background that encompasses certain assumptions regarding how a musical piece or work of sound art is supposed to be, and include the skills needed to realize or at least to approach that ideal.

And yet even if our gestures are constrained in a general sense by the skills and sense of structure that constitute them as possibilities, our relationship to them is still imbued with freedom. But these techniques and formal structures aren't realized until they are produced by the improviser's concrete gestures, which are themselves the products of choices made in the moment of improvisation. We are left the freedom to act within the complex interplay of forms and sounds that make up the developing performance. For whatever we actually play, we could always have chosen to play something different, had a different sound or phrase somehow suggested itself to us as we played. Thus our intuitive sense of form influences but doesn't determine our moment-to-moment decisions; the musical structures it encompasses exist as possibilities, not as inevitabilities.

Improvisation—Immersion—Intention

At its best, when we improvise we become immersed in the performance. This is brought out in some of the common figures of speech often used to describe that state of immersion—we say we're "lost in the music," "absorbed in the sound" or "in the zone." When all goes well and we feel we're in the zone, we're simply unaware of the background conditions that afford the possibilities our performance endeavors to realize and simply draw on what we know without reflecting on it. All we know is our immersion in the process of creation—our gestures and responses seem immediately and directly solicited by the musical situation as it unfolds from moment to moment. It isn't that we don't know what we're doing, but that we don't know that we know what we're doing. We do know, but our knowledge is not an object of particular, focused attention, it isn't something separate and distinct standing over against us as we play. Rather, this knowledge is part of the unarticulated background against which our performance takes place. We act out of a deeply rooted knowledge of what to do, but it is a knowledge immanent in the act that expresses it.

As is true of the intuitive knowledge that guides our playing, the intentions that inform our performance rarely become explicit to us as we play. The improvisational gesture may be purposive, but its purpose—the intention it is aimed toward realizing—isn't prior to the physical movement either in importance or in time. The gesture has its purpose built into it, as it were; the intention is nothing other than an embodied element of the action. Thus the improvisational gesture counts as a holistic action because the intention—that is to say, its purpose or meaning—and the action are inseparable. The intention isn't a goal reflected on and formulated prior to the act but rather is embedded in the act and is known simply as a way of being present to oneself and the situation while acting.

For purposes of analysis we can separate intention and physical action, but in real time such a distinction—which is inevitably a theoretical, after-the-fact construct—collapses into an indivisible whole. We can analyze a gesture in such a way, but only because it has become an object of reflection, a kind of opacity we construct for ourselves. This is in contrast to the way the gesture is lived in real time. We experience it simply as a way of being present to ourselves and to the situation. The gesture is an event in a sequence of events, an occurrence in a stream of occurrences in which the intention isn't a prior thing or moment that subsequently gives rise to the gesture, but is a dimension of the gesture of which it is a holistic component.

This purposive aspect of improvisation—the sense that any given musical gesture is meant, or in other words is taking place for a reason—is experienced as a kind of attunement or feeling of fit or rightness that accompanies the unfolding of the gestures within the music. We feel our gestures as appropriate responses to the musical situation as it develops around us. Thus it is that I play a certain sound or phrase or pause because I meant to, and my having done so successfully is present to me simply as a certain feeling that both accompanies and results from the gesture. This sense of fit or rightness isn't anything we stop to notice or reflect on—it isn't something we are aware of as if it were an object separate from the action in relation to which it arises—but rather is an aspect of our immersion in the music and in our part in it. Without this sense of fit or rightness we wouldn't be immersed in the improvisation; instead we'd be jolted out of it with the feeling that something had gone wrong or wasn't as it should be. At that point we might self-consciously reflect on what we're doing in order to put it right and return to our previous state of immersion in the music.

Improvisation as Self Disclosure

The holistic nature of the improvisational gesture has an important implication that goes directly to the heart of our being in the performance. To paraphrase something the philosopher and art critic Arthur Danto once wrote, when the intention to act is a contemporaneous, inseparable part of the act, the distinction between being and doing dissolves. One just is what one does.

If this is so, then improvisation entails an irreducible kind of self-disclosure on the part of the improviser; the gesture is a realization of the improviser as much as it is the impetus for the occasion of a sound. Both sides of this single action—the realization of sound and the realization of self—are inextricably bound up together in the same way that the intention and the physical movement making up the musical gesture are inextricably bound up together.

To put it in unabashedly existential terms, improvisation discloses the improviser's way of being in the world, of taking the world as a site for meaningful activity projecting toward a modification of that world. It is through the performance that we modify the world, creating a temporally-bound object that hadn't existed before. The specific form this object takes is the result of the moment-to-moment choices we make and as such it embodies our own conception of meaningful form. We can't help but create forms imbued with meaning, since through our choices we reveal the formal structures and plastic vocabulary to which we have been drawn. Each improvised gesture represents the result of a formal judgment that is our own and through which we reveal something of ourselves. With it we disclose our sense of how things should be, how the situation this moment should be resolved in this particular way.

Thus to the extent that the formal choices we make while improvising express our skills and our apprehension of the situation within which we act, we express ourselves. Consequently, there is an ineliminably expressive dimension to improvisation quite apart from whatever expression of private emotion its sounds may also embody. Seen this way, form is expressive no less than content. And there is more. Because improvisation entails real-time composition, it discloses us in a particularly unpremeditated way. We are what we disclose of ourselves in the moment, without the benefit (or drawback) of taking back what we've just done. The stakes are higher this way; every improvised action becomes a risk in that it reveals a choice of ourselves which has to stand without revision. At its most uncompromising, free improvisation is self-disclosure without regrets.

Seven Theses on "the Emotional Life of Words"

What if language expresses as much by what is between words as by words themselves? By that which it does not "say" as by what it "says"? And what if, hidden in empirical language, there is a second-order language in which signs once again lead the vague life of colors...? — Maurice Merleau-Ponty, *Signs*

In the essay "Marvelous versus Mystery," André Breton articulates what could stand as the definitive statement of Surrealist verbal poetics when he declares that:

> The emotional life of words, far from being simply contingent on their meanings, predisposes them to be drawn to one another and to make a greater impact than meaning alone, but only if they are brought together according to secret affinities that let them combine in all kinds of new ways.

In the context of the essay, Breton's declaration is an assertion of the poetic value of language in the face of what he felt was its degradation when language is taken to be no more than a medium for the conveyance of information. Breton instead envisioned a "new language" that would "be as different as possible from ordinary language," a language that would draw attention to the "emotional value of words" and away from their capacity to indicate facts and hence their potential reduction to the banal reporting of states of affairs in the external world. Breton's is an intriguing suggestion pregnant with implications not only for the practice of poetry, from which his illustrative examples derive and to which his suggestions appear to be directed, but for an understanding of the relationship of language to the language user more generally, and for what those implications might tell us of how language actually means for its users. Breton's essay, which not uncharacteristically is more impressionistic than analytical, does not for the most part tease out these implications or make explicit the assumptions that serve as their conditions for possibility. The following handful of theses are an attempt to begin doing just that, and to explore some of those possibilities as well.

Thesis No. 1:
The "emotional life of words" is a function of language as idiolectical

Language is a public thing. Languages "belong to" and are the expressions of the groups that use them. The meanings of words, and the proper way to use them, are the more-or-less stable products of the multiple intentions and uses, in the context of intragroup communication, of a community of language users. Consequently, a language is intelligible to the members of one of these groups, or language communities; its grammar is understood and its and meanings generally agreed-upon and accepted by users within the group. This public aspect or dimension of language is language as *koiné*, as something standard and held in common by a group.

What Breton's statement seems to allude to is the well-known phenomenon of language's carrying, in addition to its public meaning, meanings and/or associations particular to individual language users. Not all language users within a language community grasp meaning in exactly the same way; users assimilate language within the context of their own personal histories and encounters with other language users. The finer-grained any one language user's understanding of meaning, the more likely that understanding will carry shadings and nuances particular to that user alone. These shadings and nuances are a matter of *how* words represent rather than *what* they represent—their senses, or the aspects under which they represent their referents, which can be expected to vary within individual members of a language community. Language, in other words, has an idiolectical dimension to it. Because language as the collective property of a language community has in the end to be assimilated by individual speakers within that community, each with his or her own experiences, competences, limitations, exposures to others within the language community and so forth, language is, at the level of the individual, an idiolectical thing.

And one of the first places we might expect to find language's "secret," and presumably highly individuated, affinities would be in its idiolectical dimension.

Thesis No. 2:
Idiolectical variation is more than semantic variation

At the level of an individual's idiolect, semantic meaning—the definition of a word as understood by that individual—is in its details likely to be particular to that individual. Beyond the word's semantic or referential meaning, though, it will likely carry associations reflecting the situations in which the language user encountered the word. Individual language users' idiolects are made up of more than just variations on semantics; they are made up as well of highly personal associations incidental to, and yet permeative of, language and which overflow its narrow use as a communicative tool. These associations may connect words or other language units with images, colors, sounds, memories, scents, and so on, to form a multimodal web of significance. (What I am describing here is akin to synaesthesia, and like synaesthesia, may not be universally present among individuals in any given group of people. Perhaps this is one point at which poets and non-poets diverge.)

The "emotional life of language" that Breton celebrates, then, is to be found here, in the extra-semantic, idiolectic associations that language carries for the individual language user. Thus idiolectical variation can be found not only in *what* words mean, but in *how* they mean--in the broadest sense of meaning.

Thesis No. 3:
Idiolectical association is a form of meaning, too

Idiolectical associations aren't meanings in the semantic sense, but instead overflow semantic meanings. Nevertheless, idiolectic associations are a kind of meaning, one analogous to, but different from, semantic meaning. What they constitute is a different layer or dimension of meaning in addition to, and over and above, semantic meaning—a meaning that is a function of significance rather than reference or indication. If the measure of semantic meaning is something like the accuracy or reasonably approximate adequacy of the fit between language and the world outside of language, the measure of the meaning of significance is something else. Rather than indicating how things are in the world "outside" of us and independent of us, its focus is more reflexive, more "inwardly" directed. (The spatiallly-derived metaphors of inside and outside aren't entirely satisfactory, given the mutual dependence and mutual projection of meanings binding oneself and the world, but when kept in mind as being metaphors od convenience, they do give a sense of the contrast between these two types of meaning.)

More accurate, perhaps, would be to say that, through the idiolectical associations words and other language units carry for their individual users, meaning manifests itself as significance or alternately, that significance is the meaning words and other language units take on as they show up for us in relation to the things with which we are concerned. This relational aspect of significance is essential; significance is always significance for someone, a specific person with specific beliefs and desires, a given history and an understanding of him- or herself within his or her world. This type of meaning, in other words, is one of meaningfulness and hence—at least potentially—of affective weight rather than of descriptive or constative adequacy.

Within this expansive notion of meaning, words' meanings consist not only in what they represent, as collectively and individually understood by the member of a language community, but in the weight of associations, affective and otherwise, they carry for individual language users within that community. What Breton calls their "emotional lives," in other words, are part of their meaning for those who use them.

Thesis No. 4:
Idiolectical associations are alogical

Words or other language units may be drawn to each other—find themselves linked to each other—on the basis of their closeness within the web of a language user's idiolectical correspondences rather than their semantic adjacency or grammatical function. Such linkages would defy any logic but their own and would appear to be arbitrary; the logic driving the resulting affinities would in fact appear to be secret, as Breton asserts.

Indeed, how these alogical associations are formed is something we may never know; it is a process that may take place at a level best described as unconscious. Pace Breton, this process presumably is not the product of, or embedded in, "the" unconscious of Freudian speculation, but rather is unconscious in the simple sense of being or taking place in such a way that one is unaware of its being or taking place.

Thesis No. 5:
Some of words' "secret affinities" may be based on their aesthetic properties

So far I've suggested that idiolectical associations specific to individuals within a language community are a source of non- or extra-semantic meanings carried by words or language units, and that these associations are capable of linking words or language units in non-logical, "poetic" ways. Here I want to suggest that, as demonstrated by some kinds of typographical, sound and asemic poetry, affinities can be drawn between words and language units (or, in the case of asemic poetry, quasi-language units, although the principle remains the same), on the basis of their aesthetic qualities: their shapes or sounds (which can be spoken or simply heard with one's inner voice, when reading silently). The sheer musicality of words may draw them together regardless of their senses. Some of this musicality may be obvious to nearly anyone; some of it may be seemingly esoteric and deeply personal: an idiolectical prosody.

Thesis No. 6:
Correspondences or "affinities" may be forged at different levels of language

This is something of a corollary to the above theses. Idiolectical associations linking otherwise unrelated words or language units may emerge from different aspects or layers of language: from the ways that words represent (i.e., in their senses, or the aspects under which they represent their referents) uniquely for individual language users; from the non-semantic significances they carry for those individual users by way of their correspondences and associations; from their aesthetic qualities. Any of these aspects, alone or in combination, may provide the linkage.

Thesis No. 7:
Language discloses its "secret affinities" most naturally in poetry

In ordinary communication between language users, we would expect that individuals' idiolectical associations would play a minimal, if any role, in structuring what is said or written. The language of communication, at least in its public-facing aspect, is language as *koiné*. Breton, for his part, viewed this mundane aspect of language as a degradation of language, which could be redeemed through poetry. In an oblique allusion to Mallarmé's well-known metaphor of language as a worn coin, Breton declared that one basic principle for poetry should be that "language can and must be protected against the erosion and discoloration that result from its use for basic exchange."

And no wonder. In contrast to practical, communicative language, which presumably must be as clear and ostensibly transparent as it is possible for a mediating substance to be, poetic language, freed of the burden of plainly conveying information, can push the alogical, aesthetic, associative and affective organization of words to its forefront, much as certain kinds of music are composed on the basis of timbre rather than more conventional melodies and harmonies. In fact it's fitting that Breton raised the matter of language's "secret affinities" in the context of an essay whose main point was a measured and qualified defense of Symbolist poetry, a poetry that, in encouraging the abandonment of what Breton characterized as "the reins of common sense," opened the way toward a poetry that could approximate a music of pure timbre..

As Within So Without: The Painter as Clairvoyant

The Partial Truth of Speed

A train station at the turn of the last century: the artificial fog of smoke rising from the exhaust funnels; the projecting forms, round and angled, of steel, iron and wood in motion toward and away from each other; the rhythmic clacking of wheels on tracks; the overlapping beats of engines chuffing; the discordant harmonies of the whistles. On the platform, a confusion of movement of people shouting over the noise—shouting greetings to those who arrive, final goodbyes to those boarding and leaving.

Train travel, with its clashing surfeit of stimuli, is the setting for Umberto Boccioni's *Stati d'animo* ("states of mind"), a cycle of three paintings showing *Gli addi* ("the goodbyes"), *Quelli che vanno* ("those who leave") and *Quelli che restano* ("those who remain"). There are actually two cycles of the *Stati d'animo* paintings, one produced in 1911 and the second in 1912. The earlier set, with its almost expressionist handling of paint and color, is freer in form than the later set which, most likely reflecting Boccioni's then-recent engagement with the rigorous angularity of Cubism, is couched in a style of broken planes and multiple perspectives. It is the earlier set that I want to address here. Its freer, more nebulous style seems especially well adapted to conveying Boccioni's meaning.

The subject matter of the trilogy, centered as it apparently is on the high technology of its day, is quintessentially Futurist, one might even say stereotypically so. At one level, the paintings are quite simply about the excitement of high speed travel and the amplification of human mobility through technological means. In the first and third paintings, forms break up dynamically, first in anticipation and then in the realization of the velocity of the train as it speeds forward to its destination. In the first picture, the thickly applied streams of red and white paint suggest the fire heating the engine's boilers and the steam escaping from the funnel; a vaguely oval shape in the middle of the canvas seems to imply the cylindrical profile of the engine's boiler. Dark figures seem to emerge from the steam and general swirl of activity—presumably those waving goodbye from the platform and from inside the cars. The liquid, coiled shapes snaking across the canvas seem to embody the blurring effects of speed.

The third painting shows the train in motion from the perspective of the passengers within; horizontally-sweeping lines of blue, green, yellow and orange, looking like Divisionist dots of color thickened and stretched out, streak by the clusters of houses making up the landscape outside the car's window. Even the second painting picturing those who stay can be read as showing a certain kind of motion: the willowy, slouching appearance of the figures encodes what we might think of as the slow motion embodied in the slack, effortfully drawn-out movements of the depressed or disappointed.

A paean to speed, then? In a sense, yes. But this interpretation is informed by a more or less conventional view of Futurism as a movement preoccupied by technology and the cult of speed—the "*nuova religione-morale della velocità*" proclaimed in F. T. Marinetti's 1916 manifesto of that name. And although true, it is a partial truth. For what Boccioni is trying to depict are, as the title explicitly claims, the thoughts and states of mind of people on the platform, in the passenger compartments, or leaving the station to return to their homes. The Futurist preoccupation with the modern technology of travel is there, but merely as a surface phenomenon; this is a picture of internal states projecting out onto, and commingled with, the external world.

Painting the Numinous World

Just a decade before *Stati d'animo* was painted, a curious book titled *Thought-forms* was published in England. The book purported to show the colors and shapes of states of mind as seen clairvoyantly by the authors, two leading members of the Theosophical Society in London, Annie Besant and Charles W. Leadbeater. Besant and Leadbeater claimed that thoughts and emotions generated forms of specific shapes and colors corresponding to the types and intensities of the mental activities that caused them. Visible only to clairvoyants, these thought forms would literally color the world with psychic energy. Besant and Leadbeater's book was a catalogue of exemplary thought forms and contained a series of color plates, produced by three artists under the authors' direction, which purported to show thought forms the authors observed. These illustrations were to exert a significant influence on early abstract painters—most notably Wassily Kandinsky—as well as other artists.

How direct an influence *Thought-forms* may have had on Boccioni is an interesting question. We know that Theosophy generally, and *Thought-forms* specifically, played influential roles in the Futurist world; in Florence and elsewhere, there was much overlap between Futurist and Theosophical circles. The French translation of *Thought-forms*, published in 1905, was quickly taken up by the Italian spiritual and artistic avant-gardes; it's possible that Boccioni had read it and had drawn inspiration from it.

Certainly, there is a resonance between the ideas and even some of the illustrations of *Thought-forms* and the subject matter and look of *Stati d'animo*—a family resemblance that tells of relation with hints of direct descent.

Whether or not he was directly influenced by *Thought-forms*, Boccioni, like Besant and Leadbeater, imagined a physical world enveloped or intersected by a numinous world full of unseen yet present psychic forces and energies accessible to the adept. It was a world that Boccioni envisaged as the real subject matter for Futurist painting. This becomes rather clear in the lecture he gave to the Circolo Artistico in Rome on 29 May 1911. In the course of his remarks, Boccioni laid out a program for Futurist painting as he saw it; the key to his program was the idea that the Futurist painter would have to be a clairvoyant of sorts—a *pittore veggente*, or painter-seer.

Overall, Boccioni makes a case for painting as a variety of clairvoyance in which feelings and sensations are depicted directly, though the mediumship of the artist. The artist is able to exercise a "Futurist hypersensibility" that operates as a kind of sixth sense, allowing that artist to "see" or sense the vibrations given off by people's states of mind; these vibrations consequently form the subject matter of the painting.

In fact, Boccioni is quite explicit that the subject matter of Futurist painting—its "nucleus"—consists in "musical forms, spiritual volume, and the *state of mind*" and not in the depiction of the "physical appearance in action" of the various modern technologies and their users. Through Futurist painting, "[t]he human eye will see colors as feelings materialized." In short, if "solid bodies give rise to states of mind by means of vibration of forms, then we will draw these vibrations." In the notes he prepared for the lecture, Boccioni quite directly set out what might be considered the programmatic statement of task for the Futurist painter: "What needs to be painted is not the visible but what has hitherto been held to be invisible, that is, what the clairvoyant painter sees."

The object of painting wouldn't be to depict the surfaces of things, but rather to show the spiritual or psychological reality invisible to the eye: to illustrate, in effect, the moods and emotions—the affective states—that permeate and help constitute the concrete reality of human experience.

Color, Line and Affect

Boccioni's formal means for depicting states of mind rely on the deft handling of color and line. To begin with the colors: the muted, monochromatic green-blue palette of *Quelli che restano*, noted above, powerfully conveys a sense of melancholy or depression. The world seen through a melancholy or depressed eye can seem devoid of coloristic subtlety or variety; all washes out into an undifferentiated, dull shade. The painting's association of a mood with a particular color is congruent with Besant and Leadbeater's cataloguing of the emotional states, some of them quite specific and finely distinguished, associated with particular shades of color. Interestingly, Besant and Leadbeater attribute sympathy to the green-blue sample they present in a table at the beginning of the book; for Boccioni, on the other hand, the green-blue he uses communicates a much more inward sense of being enclosed in one's own thoughts.

The importance of line to Boccioni's rendering of emotion we know from the artist's own statements. He described his method in some detail in the preface to an exhibition of Futurist work shown first at the Bernheim-Jeune gallery in Paris in February 1912, and later at the 1915 Panama-Pacific Exhibition in San Francisco. Although the preface was signed by several Futurist painters, Boccioni was most likely responsible for most of it; he almost certainly was responsible for this:

> We thus arrive at what we call the *painting of states of mind*.
>
> In the pictorial description of the various states of mind of a leave-taking, perpendicular lines, undulating and as it were worn out, clinging here and there to silhouettes of

> empty bodies, may well express languidness and discouragement.
>
> Confused and trepidating lines, either straight or curved, mingled with the outlined hurried gestures of people calling one another, will express a sensation of chaotic excitement.
>
> On the other hand, horizontal lines, fleeting, rapid, and jerky, brutally cutting into half-lost profiles of faces or crumbling and rebounding fragments of landscape, will give the tumultuous feelings of the persons going away.

Boccioni's translation of affective lines of force into the painterly language of color and linear form is accomplished with a directness and forcefulness. The boundaries between colors are defined and yet permeable, implying a mutual influence or exchange of affective energy among the scene's participants.

Take, for example, the thickly-textured *Gli addi*. The scene is rendered in an agitated swirl of viscous waves of muddy reds, blacks and teal blues. The dark colors predominate and give the painting a certain heaviness—the heaviness of preoccupation, of thoughts of impending separation. In *Quelli che vanno*, dynamically sweeping lines of blue and green-blue interspersed with yellow and orange are set at an angle suggesting swift movement from right to left. These signs of velocity rake over a view of the landscape outside the train window, a scene of buildings jumbled and askew as seen from the perspective of the speeding train. And finally there is *Quelli che restano* with its dark, slouching ghostly figures dissolving into a vertical haze of semi-transparent, serpentine lines of pale green and yellow-green.The cumulative effect of the three paintings of the *Stati d'animo* group is of an experience of emotion as something that engulfs one, that literally colors one's apprehension of the surrounding world.

Boccioni's handling of plastic forms does convey the notion of a world shot through with forces invisible to the ordinary eye. In claiming to depict a world permeated by invisible energies and vibrations, he could further claim that he wasn't portraying anything that recent scientific discoveries hadn't revealed or implied. This was a common idea at the time among contemporary occultists. The invisible forces and correspondences Besant, Leadbeater and others claimed to see at work in the world were often likened to such recently discovered or theorized physical phenomena as electromagnetic force, X-rays and radioactivity. Roentgen's discovery of X-rays, for example, was particularly intriguing to occultists, for these invisible rays that could pass through matter offered proof of an unseen reality that could be corroborated and described in scientific terms, and thus would support their own speculations concerning unseen levels of reality.

And just as X-rays had been detected by scientific experiment, the energies and emanations claimed by occultists were expected ultimately to be apprehended and accepted by science as well: today's occult claim would be tomorrow's scientifically established fact. In fact many scientists of the time, including chemist Sir William Crookes and physicist Sir Oliver Lodge, belonged to associations interested in occult phenomena or undertook investigations of claimed occult manifestations. It's hardly surprising that Besant and Leadbeater could —and did—claim a kinship between their occult investigations and the advanced scientific thinking of the day. Boccioni and like-minded artists were no different.

For Boccioni, X-rays provided an example of the amplification of ordinary perception—a looking through matter that for all practical purposes represented a kind of sixth sense analogous to the clairvoyant powers the occultists and Futurists alike claimed to possess. In the April, 1910 *Technical Manifesto* of Futurist painting, Boccioni, along with his coauthors, explicitly drew a parallel between the Futurist painter's clairvoyance and the penetrating revelations of the X-rays. If X-rays made the invisible visible, they provided an appropriate trope for the Futurists' "multiplied sensibility" which, they claimed in their *Technical Manifesto*, allowed them to "intuit the obscure manifestations of mediumistic phenomena...with results analogous to those of X-rays."

What this intuition revealed was a deeper reality in which the solid bodies of plain vision were revealed to be nothing other than "condensed atmospheres," as Boccioni described them in the Rome Lecture, and apparently empty spaces were in fact traversed by the vibrations of ethereal substances given off by thought, sensation and affect. The X-ray-like vision of the painter-seer did nothing more than reveal this deeper reality undergirding visible reality, which he would then conjure in strokes of paint on canvas.

A World of Emotional Shadows

The Futurist painter as seer—as *pittore veggente*--would, it seems, transpose the psychological realities of the affective states through which the world is disclosed into the material language of painted forms. And Boccioni's trilogy very neatly puts this theory into practice. Through their play of colors and forms, the paintings depict a world filtered through—literally colored by—the emotional responses it elicits. This may explain in part the Futurist predilection for portraying events or objects provocative of strong emotion or stress: riots, battles, bodies in rapid motion precariously poised at the edge of control. But what of the ostensibly more mundane experience of travel?

As used to them as we may be, the occasions and locations associated with travel—by train or any other means—naturally continue to elicit powerful emotions. The scenes of departure, separation and passage that provide Boccioni with his starting point are scenes of deep emotional meaning for those involved. Thus what Boccioni is attempting to depict, in an explicit way, are the specific emotional meanings that the train station and its network of relationships hold for the people passing through it. These latter occupy different positions within a network of actions and emotions, largely on the basis of what they are doing at the moment and where they are destined to be: leaving to go elsewhere, or staying. The position one holds within that network of action casts the moment of departure in a certain emotional light.

Those who stay may be seen to be in a disappointed state of immobility, of literally being left behind and consequently left out of the dynamic adventure of hurtling into the future at speed. Those who leave, by contrast, participate in the thrill of forward motion, of actively pushing forward into a future whose inevitable approach is quickened by modern technology. Relative to those who leave, those left behind are quite simply left—abandoned by those who have departed.

Stripped of any occult claims to clairvoyance and seership, Boccioni's paintings, along with his program of seership more generally, offers an insight into the way that emotion and mood function as cognitive elements in the human engagement with the world. His series delivers an insight into the way emotional states disclose and at the same time constitute our world as being a certain way for us, as having a certain value. The world takes on structures and significance through our preoccupations, expectations, reservations, attractions and aversions; we organize it according to what we see in it, need from it, expect of it—and whether or not any of those meanings, needs and expectations are met.

The affective response that a place, person or event elicits is thus in essence a judgment rendered, a judgment concerning our understanding of it as mattering to us in a concrete way. Through our affective responses the world is grasped as being-for-us in a way particular to us at that particular moment. As a cognitive tool, affective judgment doesn't supplant rational judgment so much as supplement it; through affect, judgment is transposed from the universal to the particular, from a matter of abstract reason to a matter of the world as concretely lived by a really existing person. If it reveals our reality as made up of indifferent matter, it is indifferent matter we are unable to be indifferent to.

By showing states of mind as being projected out into the world, Boccioni captures another truth about them: they bind us to the world. Affective states may have their sources within us, but at the same time they direct us outward to the world around us—a world they disclose to us as concerning us. They effectively anchor us within a network of relationships that are partly of their own making. We may not literally emanate vibrations to weave a web enmeshing our environment and the people and things within it, but we do—to change metaphors—cast our emotional shadows and let them fall all around us.

A Realism of Occult Correspondences

Boccioni's trilogy, then, is a rendering of experiences rather than of events or objects as such. As a consequence, each canvas represents a synthetic unity of the various emotions surrounding the station, the train and those caught up in the drama of travel. Through this unity there arises a kind of super realism—a realism enhanced by an apprehension of the fundamental reality behind the superficial reality of appearances. Not the realism of empirical facts and the visible material world alone, but rather what Luciano Chessa has aptly called "the occult realism of the simultaneity of states of consciousness." It is an anti-materialist realism that takes the plain sensual world as the occasion for and symbol of the occult reality that surrounds it; it is a realism of occult correspondences, of psychological states rather than objective facts.

The correspondences encoded in these paintings are correspodences in which the analogy is drawn between the external world and the internal, psychological world as revealed by the purportedly clairvoyant painter. As described in the preface to the Bernheim-Jeune show, the clairvoyant painter

> seek[s] by intuition the sympathies and links which exist between the exterior (concrete) scene and the interior (abstract) emotion. Those lines, those spots, those zones of color, apparently illogical and meaningless, are the mysterious keys to our pictures.

In Boccioni's occult super-realism, the hard and fast line separating the subjective from the objective—the experience from the experienced—is shown to be in fact a permeable tissue; we are always already outside of ourselves, emotionally involved in the world at the same time that the world is in a sense within us, as an element of our self-conscious and psychological environment.

Thus the role of the train. For all its mechanized power, it plays a symbolic role based on something other than standing as a totem of technological transformation. To depict it isn't simply to transcribe its external features—its metal skin, sleek angles and moving parts—but to penetrate into what the Futurists would hold is its occult reality. This latter consists in its symbolic function, its function as a term in an equation of correspondences between the material, external world and the world of projected meanings. In this equation of correspondences, the train is a variable whose revealed value consists in its capacity to signify the spiritualization of matter. It was, as Marinetti declared in *La nuova religione-morale della velocità,* "inhabited by the divine." The Futurist fascination with the machine and technology thus doesn't represent a fetishization of technology per se; rather, it was the outward projection of an interest in technical advance as the symbol of human creativity, as the objective-correlate of the spirit. As expressed by the Futurists Enrico Prampolini, Ivo Panaggi and Vinicio Paladini in the manifesto *L'arte meccanica*, the machine is "the most exuberant symbol of the mysterious human creative force." As such, it was the signifier of a meaning that it embodied and yet that surpassed it at the same time.

Within the Futurist system of correspondences, the machine resolves the apparent contradiction between the material and spiritual by standing as an objective symbol of the deeper reality of the will that called it into being in the first place. Here human will finds its analogue in its own products—in the technology that its creativity gives rise to. The Futurist fascination with simultaneity can also be seen as assuming the correspondence not only between the coincidences of multiple physical bodies in motion, but also, and more significantly, between the coincidences of multiple emotional states—the unseen events and sensations, experienced by multiple people, as revealed to, and subsequently depicted by, the *pittore veggente*. And it is with this correspondence that Futurism for all practical purposes takes the old Hermetic formula, As Above, So Below and responds with a counter-formula: As Within, So Without.

Joëlle Léandre: Being with Sound

For over forty years—since playing a solo set in Buffalo, New York in 1976—French double bassist Joëlle Léandre has been bringing a uniquely forceful and personal kind of improvised music to life. Whether alone or with others, she plays with a polymorphously full engagement, inhabiting the performance as a good actor would inhabit a character. But it isn't a kind of musical method acting; rather, it's her way—a perfectly natural way, and one arising of its own accord—of directing the full force of her personality into the substance of her craft. As she does as well with interviews and in her autobiography.

Training and Chance, Freedom and Discipline

Several years ago there appeared through the Kadima Collective, a group dedicated to improvised and free musics, a small book. The book, issued as part of a triple package including a CD and DVD, is Léandre's autobiography, as written in conversation with Franck Medioni. Originally published in French as *A voix basse*, it was translated into English as *Solo*. An artist's account of his or her own work, and the life events that surrounded and formed it can, by definition, provide a revelatory insight into how a particular art is the way it is; in the case of an artist given to self-awareness, such an account can, in addition to illuminating the creative process, bring to light as well creative motivation and with it the rare insight into the why as well as the how behind the art. Léandre is nothing if not a self-aware artist, as *Solo* shows throughout.

The first thing that comes through in the book is the grain of the voice, as a living presence. This is very much an oral autobiography, which crackles with all the immediacy and spontaneity of having the subject herself in the room, speaking directly to the reader. Like her definition of jazz, the conversation recorded is a ceaselessly creative effusion stamped with her personality: outspokenly passionate, impulsive, and often blunt in expression. The book is structured topically, allowing her to situate events of her life story in the context of her thoughts on her background and education, influences, instrument, and approach to improvisation.

Léandre comes from a working class family in the south of France. Indeed, a recurring motif of the book is her conception, clearly drawn from her own self-conception, of the musician as a worker or an artisan as much as an artist—or, to use one of her images, as a farmer who gets up early every morning and gets to work with his tractor. A strong work ethic figures prominently in the stories she tells—of studies with Pierre Delescluse and following that at the Paris Conservatoire, and of her own early practice regimen. Although it can be said that her subsequent career in improvisation involved the renunciation of some aspects of her grounding in European art music, she does credit her rigorous training with giving her a solid foundation in technique and reading ability that allowed her access not only to some of the most advanced literature for her instrument, but to a deep grasp of its possibilities and limits. This foundation is still evident in Léandre's characteristic blend of the structures and sound palette of contemporary art music with the energy and spontaneity of jazz.

As important as her formal training was, of equal importance was a set of chance encounters and of more deliberate meetings with remarkable men and women. One such encounter was with a recording—a Slam Stewart LP Léandre picked up in 1971, because she liked its cover. The music, which she describes as a "shock to the system," introduced her to jazz and broadened her relationship to the bass. Of the significant people she met—among them Giacinto Scelsi, Derek Bailey, Cecil Taylor, George Lewis, Anthony Braxton and Irene Schweizer-several were to exert influence over her music as well as her more general outlook on life. One of the most important of these people was John Cage, whom she first met during her initial trip to the United States in 1976. Cage opened her up to sound as such; his advice to her to let sounds be themselves had a profound philosophical as well as musical impact on her, and contributed to her decision to be more than just an orchestral or ensemble bassist. From Cage, whom she describes as her "spiritual father," she got a sense of freedom and the permission to follow it. It's easy to see how Cage's philosophy of freedom conjoined to discipline would be congenial to her, appealing as it does to both sides of her character—her work ethic and her impulsiveness. Léandre's relationship to Cage was such that she suggested he write a score for double bass; his response was *Ryoanji*, which as she tells it was conceived in Marcel Duchamp's apartment in Neuilly, where Cage frequently stayed when visiting France.

"A Big Empty Box"

The double bass is a singular instrument. Just considered as a brute physical object, it is imposing in sheer scale and mass. Its size can vary, ranging from the relatively small ¼ size through the common 3/4 size to the six-foot tall full size, but with its broad shoulders and hips, it always manages to give an impression of bulk. It's also something of a shape-shifter, coming as it does in different body types—gamba, violin-cornered, busetto—reflecting its obscure origins as a descendent of the viols that, somewhere along the way, determined to become a hybrid and consequently acquired some of its features from the violin family as well. Its range grounds it in the musical fundamentum, giving it a sonic weight reinforced by an overtone structure that favors the lower harmonics and renders its tones in darker colors. To those who don't know it well, the instrument can take on the guise of a lumbering creature, a Minotaur wandering a labyrinth spun of its own sound. But that's just one of its personae—a chosen mask rather than an inherent trait resistant to change. It can also speak with delicacy in a modulated voice not rising above a stage whisper.

Despite its physical ungainliness and a compass biased toward the low end of the pitch spectrum, the double bass has an expressive range both exceptional and exceptionally agile. The depth of its natural voice under the bow or when plucked is familiar to virtually anyone who's heard any kind of Western music, but it also has an extended voice, or rather, voices, encompassing thin, flute-like harmonics; complex multiphonics; the brittle staccato of strings plucked behind the stop; the hollow, wind-like sounds of the bridge being bowed; the quiet rumble of the bowed tailpiece; and more. Its range of sounds is seemingly limited only by the imagination, tempered by skill, of the player.

Léandre's relationship to this versatile, if occasionally intransigent, instrument reflects a long-standing and deep engagement with it in light of its potential as both vehicle and obstacle for those who play it. What seems to attract her is the intense physicality associated with playing the bass as well as the sonorous quality of its voice. *Solo*'s chapter "Base/Bass" may well be the finest description, from the first-person point of view, of the bass-bassist symbiosis—of what it's like to live with and through one of these large wooden monsters. The bass for Léandre is a second body, "a big empty box" supported in every sense by the musician who must play it in spite of the difficulties inherent in its large size and limited portability. (Any double bassist will nod in agreement when she describes the bass as a "whopping great thing that puts us through hell. But we love it.") One gets the impression that more so than many, if not most, instrumentalists, Léandre's connection to her instrument resembles the connection one has to one's own body—a self-presence prior to reflection and the consequent making of oneself into an object separate from, and standing outside of, one's awareness. Such a self-presence can be a source of pleasure, frustration, exhilaration, fatigue, want and satiety. To that extent the bass does seem to be like an extension of the body for her—an apparently transparent presence in which the instrument as mediator of the player's impulse is virtually subsumed by, and made a part of, the impulse. As with the relationship to oneself, it is a relationship that leaves no room for neutrality. One is engaged—one must be engaged—passionately, in a visceral way.

We can see and hear this passionate engagement, and it all it means in terms of improvisational dynamics, in Léandre's live performances. Take, for example, a 28 November, 2016 solo performance at the Eglise Saint-Eustache, an event held to mark the fortieth anniversary of Léandre's career in creative music. Its seven-and-a-half minutes unfold as an ongoing argument between the instrumentalist and the instrument—an uninhibited exchange where each side knows precisely what to say and where to go in order to provoke the other to the greatest extent, which is exactly what would happen during any argument between longtime intimate partners. Léandre puts her entire body into it, sliding her fingers up and down the fingerboard, striking open strings against stopped strings, strumming chords, tapping the table and ribs, hammering and pulling with her left hand while the right bows with a rapid pulse. She extracts as many shadings of tone as the instrument is willing to let her have; as with so many of her performances, this one is driven by timbral change and rhythmic forward motion, a differential system of sound colors that develops through a sequence of contrasts. And throughout, she keeps up a vocal counter-argument—full-throated one minute, *sotto voce* the next, and all played with and against the line emerging from the bass.

Sound Over Virtuosity

One of the most revealing moments in *Solo* comes when Léandre asserts that she's chosen to pursue sound over virtuosity. It is an important decision that informs her playing and one that also represents a choice based on a recognition of the concrete possibilities open to her. It is an important choice in that in choosing it, Léandre chooses herself as an artist; such a choice seems to embody the understanding that we define ourselves as much by our possibilities as by the choices that those possibilities make possible, since possibility is just the future choice that has yet to be made. In choosing sound over virtuosity, Léandre has made it her own basic project as an artist to cultivate the distinct features of her instrument in its entirety; not only that, but to cultivate a certain standpoint in relation to the instrument —a co-partnership based on a recognition of the instrument's unique features and capabilities, an acknowledgment of its physical presence as a complex object made of wood and strung with metal, reacting in appropriately complex ways to the artist's hand.

Léandre's choice of sound over virtuosity has ramifications beyond her own playing, though. It serves as an example to other bassists, and to improvisers generally, opening up to them the possibility of establishing a deliberately fundamental relationship to their instruments and to improvisation itself. This is because sound is the fulcrum on which every musician balances. Our engagement with our instrument begins with sound and in the end returns to sound; whatever else we bring—our musical vocabulary and syntax, our expressive goals and renunciations—is built on a foundation of the sound we are able to draw. The more solid the foundation the more that can be built on top of it—and paradoxically, the less that needs to be built. Sound by itself can speak with a unique eloquence; this seems to be what Léandre is driving at. Beyond this, sound is the material trace of the uniqueness of the voice, the signature by which we as musicians recognize each other and ultimately, ourselves. Our sound conveys us, carries our meaning at the same time that it colors our meaning, making color an inextricable part of our meaning. Sound is to our playing as prosody is to our speaking: the how of what is said rather than the what. To understand this is to understand that it is as much through the how that we grasp the what. Under the best circumstances, sound is our temperament made audible.

Sound is also a direct indicator of our interface with the instrument. Sound—whether refined or coarse, rounded or sharp-edged, sensual or austere, full-bodied or meager—is that quality of what we play as it is brought out specifically by our touch. To that extent, sound is in the hands. When someone is fighting against the instrument we can hear it; when the player and instrument have made their peace with each other and have even come to a more than grudging understanding of each other, we can hear that too. (Our hands remind us that the instrument is the object as matter, an inert plenitude at once facilitating and rubbing up against our efforts to convey or construct something with it.) Léandre seems to know this instinctively, and it may be that, given the physical challenges involved in playing the bass, it would take a bassist to put sound at the center of her music.

In sum, to focus on one's sound is to foreground an awareness of the relationship one has with one's instrument, to recognize the role of touch not only in expressing one's meaning, but ultimately in developing an idiom that effectively reflects one's musical sensibility. There again, it's temperament made audible, through the mediation of the hand.

Response and Receptivity

In addition to their musicality, Léandre's performances are notable for the element of theatricality she often brings to them. As with the Eglise Saint-Eustache performance, it isn't unusual for her to integrate voice and movement into the music, creating a multi-modal experience of particular richness. Seemingly more than most, she incorporates a gesturality in her work that goes beyond the effort needed for the mere production of sound. In this regard it is interesting to read that she comes from a family of circus clowns—and it's easy to see the connection between the clown, relying on the eloquence of gesture and an expressive motility, and the bassist herself, who draws on these same resources in performance.

Léandre's theatricality may be unusual, but it can't be written off as an eccentricity of hers, or as a distracting side effect of what she needs to do in order to make music. On the contrary, it would seem instead to be close to the main point of the music, a point consisting in the determined projecting out of herself through the material—the material of the instrument, the musical material as it is improvised, and ultimately the material presence of the body engaging with its surroundings: responding to the resistance of the instrument, the flux of the music, the active presence of others both performing and witnessing the performance.

Her theatricality rounds out the performance, inserts her more fully into it and shows it to be the "complete opening" out that she has said she takes improvisation, ideally, to entail. Her theatricality represents a form of receptivity as well as a way of projecting herself by enacting a role onstage.

Ideally improvisation, and especially improvisation in the absence of predetermined or premeditated structures, is built on receptivity. Over the course of the improvisation structures will form, but the improviser has to listen for them and be guided as much by what their logic seems to entail and what their momentum seems to predict as by what direction he or she wishes to give them.

The implications are musical, but they go beyond music narrowly defined and open out toward the existential dimension of improvisation—the dimension through which we become aware of being in a situation presenting us with certain possibilities, some of which we have created in the moment, some of which are embedded in the background we bring to the situation, and on the basis of all of which we must act.

Through a receptivity attuned to that awareness, the improviser integrates sequential points of experience, makes sense of them not only as emergent musical structures but as moments carrying meaning for, and reflecting the engagements of, oneself, one's fellow performers, and one's audience. Receptivity grasps the accumulation of these moments as a situation in formation, as something of concern eliciting a response. How one chooses to respond goes to the heart of improvisation. For Léandre, the response is one to which she brings all of herself. She's described improvisation as something that "wakes and reveals" ("*révèle et reveille*," in the more mellifluous French); but by itself, revelation isn't enough—at the very least, it must be recognized as such if it is to have any effect. Revelation succeeds or fails by virtue of the degree of receptivity of the person to whom it is made—the degree of "wakefulness."

Receptivity, though, is one moment within a larger dialectic whose complementary moment is projection. For Léandre, an important element of improvisation is a projection of what she is as well as what she knows how to play or what she actually does play—these latter ultimately being at the service of the former. Like all of us, she's a rounded human being; more so than many improvisers, she makes this fact a substantial part of what she conveys through her performance. Over the course of one of her sets she's apt to project herself in many ways: as playful, serious, passionate, engaging, self-conscious, bothered—as being in any of a number of different kinds of state of mind.

But above all, she projects herself as someone with a sense of humor. Humor for her is a mode of action as well as a quality of the act: to follow one of her improvisations over its course is to witness the arc of humor at play—the set-up, the build, the deliberate sense of timing that delays release until the moment it's most needed. None of this is an inevitable effect of improvisation—it must be chosen. In making this choice, Léandre has consciously situated herself within a tradition of what she calls the "desacralization of the serious," a tradition that reaches backward to Dada and forward to the performance art of Joseph Beuys.

Although she often plays solo and has performed in ensembles of different sizes, Léandre plays quite frequently in duets. The format seems to suit her musically, as is brought out in her vast discography: she's recorded duets with, among many others, Anthony Braxton; George Lewis; percussionist Mark Nauseef; pianists Masahiko Sato and Yuji Takahashi; vocalist Lauren Newton; violinist India Cook; saxophonist Phillip Greenlief—an eclectic group of partners reflecting her willingness to meet others on a spontaneously-created common ground. In any given duet, one can hear this ground in the process of its formation: the dynamic between Léandre and her partner is always palpable, a pulling-at and pushing-against, a playing with and through the resistance of the other voice, the moments of concord and discord that reproduces, within the semi-artificial setting of stage and studio, the fraught interactions between two different human beings—metaphorically it could be any two human beings, not just these particular performers—encountering each other as confluent and competing projects sharing a situation, as sheer presences amplifying, subsuming and refracting each other under the pressure of a common set of circumstances in pursuit of congruent ends. The improvised duet is, in effect, a universe of two held together by the tensions of centripetal and centrifugal forces.

Because it only involves two partners, the improvised duet tends to lay bare the mechanics of interaction through which an improvisation is accomplished. To an attuned witness, the improvised duet heightens the perceptibility of a certain creative tension inherent in improvisation as an activity. As an artistic creation, the improvisation is an object other than and standing over against the improvisers who create it. Yet each improviser internalizes it by apprehending it in his or her own way, as a phenomenon or appearance that he or she then engages as something to be shaped, extended, modified, and finally truncated and completed in real time. This object-phenomenon relationship holds in any improvisation whether solo or for large ensemble, but when two improvisers are involved, the improvisation as an unfolding system of similarities and differences based on similar and contrasting choices that themselves are the product of responses to similar and contrasting appearances, is thrown into stark relief. The corollary is that in the relatively simple setting of the duet, the personalities of the improvisers are more dramatically revealed through their reception of the improvisation and their consequent responses to it.

Léandre is particularly suited to the duet because her outlook is essentially humanist, and one feels, in hearing her duet recordings or watching them on video, that it is the confrontation at the level of the human that interests her as much as the prospect of creating a satisfying musical experience. She's said in interviews that she prefers the duet for its intimacy and for the possibilities it opens up for a substantive relationship—for an authentic exchange of perspectives no matter how temporary or no matter how ostensibly mismatched the partnership. It is an exchange not only between performers, but between people, each of whom is shaped by a history, by desires and beliefs, possibilities and limitations.

Beyond any fellow performers, though, for Léandre there would always seem to be another partner in this music: the listener. She has said that she feels it's her responsibility as an artist to communicate with the listener, to touch him or her and ultimately to convey something of the freedom she feels is at the heart of life, if only we can find it. And in the end it would seem to be this faith in the listener—in the listener's capacity to hear and through hearing to be transformed, to realize a certain freedom he or she may not be aware of already possessing or being possessed by, and through that realization to accept an invitation to reinvent him or herself—that grounds her music. Against the common perception that fully improvised music is difficult or in some way esoteric, Léandre asserts that it's really for everybody. And ideally it is: for anybody who can open to up to someone wishing to speak directly to them.

The Anti-Metaphysical Metaphysician

The School That Was Not a School

January, 1917. Italy was entering the third year of its involvement in the First World War. The Piedmontese painter Carlo Carrà, now a soldier in the Italian army's 27th Infantry Regiment, was stationed in Pieve di Cento, outside of Ferrara. Corporal Giorgio de Chirico, also of the 27th Infantry, was already in Ferrara, working as a clerk at the army depot there. De Chirico had been in Ferrara not long after having returned to Italy from Paris in 1915 for army service. Ferrara, as it turned out, was the locus of a powerful convergence of artistic forces, and one that coincided with a significant turning point in Carrà's art.

Sometime in March, 1917, Carrà met de Chirico and de Chirico's brother Alberto Savinio. This had happened after he had initiated correspondence with them on the recommendation of journalist Giovanni Papini. In early April, both Carrà and de Chirico were sent to the army's neurological hospital in the Villa del Seminario outside of Ferrara, where they stayed until mid-August. There they painted, encouraged by the facility's director, and formed a close but short-lived partnership.

The Villa del Seminario collaboration was the core of the so-called *scuola metafisica*—the group of painters who took inspiration from de Chirico's Ferrarese paintings. In addition to de Chirico and Carrà, these painters included Giorgio Morandi and Filippo de Pisis. It was a short-lived school that wasn't really a school at all; as Giuliano Briganti points out, there was no program, no manifesto or other collective statement of purpose to define or constrain it. These were different artists with different goals but with some commonalities, among them an interest in exploring the plastic and atmospheric possibilities of depicting interior spaces containing certain kinds of objects in strange combinations.

Carrà's direct involvement with de Chirico was especially brief. He left Villa del Seminario on leave in mid-August, 1917 and shortly thereafter was honorably discharged from the army. He returned to Milan, where in December he organized an exhibition of his new paintings; de Chirico, under the impression that the show would include paintings of his own, sent Carrà three canvases, which were not included. By early 1918 the two had fallen out over what the de Chirico scholar Paolo Baldacci characterizes as Carrà's betrayal of de Chirico. While Carrà maintained that de Chirico sent his work too late to be included, Baldacci's own research into contemporary postmarked documents establishes that that wasn't the case. Either way, the collaboration, and friendly relations, between the two painters was over.

It may have been that Carrà's metaphysical period simply represented a transition for him. Since 1910, he had been a Futurist painter but by 1914 was becoming disillusioned with the movement generally and with its leader F. T. Marinetti and fellow painter Umberto Boccioni in particular. Although he continued to sign his paintings as a Futurist through 1917, he'd grown dissatisfied with the Futurist preoccupation with constant motion and disruption and was looking for what he hoped would be a way to engage the world more deeply.

For this, he felt he needed a formal language different from Futurism's fragmentary, multiplied figures. He was looking to the Italian old masters for a new direction, publishing essays on Giotto and Uccello in the art journal *La Voce* in 1916. (And in doing so pulling off a double negation: negation of the Futurist negation of the past.) His paintings, inspired by their art and the art of the Trecento, began to take on a simpler, quasi-primitive style with a deliberate coarseness or ugliness that the title of one 1916 painting seemed to sum up: *Anti-grazioso*, or "anti-graceful."

If the art of the Trecento provided one model for Carrà's turn away from Futurism, de Chirico's painting provided another. Carrà may first have seen de Chirico's paintings during a trip to Paris with Papini and his fellow critic and art journalist Ardengo Soffici in spring, 1914. It's also possible that he saw several photographs of de Chirico's work in 1916. Paolo Fossati describes Carrà's early reaction to de Chirico's pictures as "perplexed;" Baldacci reports that in a February, 1917 letter to Soffici Carrà remarked on what struck him as the "cold, literary rationalization" of de Chirico's work. But he would soon find these perplexing pictures by the younger, relatively less-established painter —de Chirico, who was then virtually unknown in Italy, would be 29 in 1917, while Carrà would be 36—to be an inspiration.

Given the situation in which Carrà found himself when he formed his alliance with de Chirico, it's fair to ask how committed he actually was to the metaphysical aesthetic and outlook. Baldacci, for his part, sees the *scuola metafisica* as something of a fiction and Carrà's part in particular to have been an opportunistic move. And at one level it does seem that much of Carrà's Ferrarese work is strikingly like one person trying to speak in another's dialect. The iconography and even some of the compositional structures are often directly borrowed from the work de Chirico had been producing since 1915. At another level, though, Carrà does seem to have been searching for a visual poetics that would let him convey what he saw as a deeper reality. And as it happened, his idea of what constituted metaphysics differed from de Chirico's.

The Metaphysics of the Ordinary

In the catalogue to his December, 1917 show in Milan, Carrà described his art as deriving from a metaphysical vision. Statements he composed in 1918 which were collected and published in the book *Pittura metafisica* in 1919 introduced and developed his notion of what metaphysical painting was concerned with and how it could create its effects. What these statements demonstrate isn't that Carrà never really was the metaphysician he claimed to be but rather that he was a somewhat paradoxical one—a peculiar kind of anti-metaphysical metaphysician who looked at things precisely *as* things.

Carrà's attitude toward things qua things is clearly articulated in a 1918 statement titled *Della 'cose ordinarie'*--"Of 'Ordinary Things.'" With it, Carrà set out a program that neatly summed up the anti-metaphysical metaphysics of the Ferrara period.

In his statement, Carrà posited ordinary things as serving as both an artistic anchor and a fundamental way of orienting oneself in the world, warning that to abandon them is to "collapse into the absurd, and thus into nothingness whether plastically or spiritually." For Carrà it was ordinary things that "reveal that form of simplicity that speaks to us of a superior state of being, which constitutes the splendid secret of art." Ordinary things may be ordinary, but their effect, for Carrà, was anything but; it's worth noting that throughout the statement the phrase "ordinary things" always appears in quotation marks, as if to call attention to the ironic fact that they aren't all that ordinary after all, their appearances and our being habituated to them to the contrary. It is here, if anywhere, that the metaphysical dimension to Carrà's artistic vision discloses itself. But because it is so rooted in the plain forms of the mundane and the material, it is a metaphysics that reveals itself through an ontological predisposition for the concrete that, in its validation of actually existing things, can only be termed anti-metaphysical. True, the "superior state of being" hinted at by the simple forms of ordinary things might possibly be identified with the hypothetical, and paradigmatically metaphysical, Platonic realm of pure form, but for Carrà access to that realm, if indeed that was what he had in mind, could only be had by way of material things.

If Carrà concerned himself with ordinary things, he did not take a stance toward them that would reduce them to their ordinary uses. On the contrary, that he was trying to show things apart from their uses is made explicit in the disdain he displayed, in "Of 'Ordinary Things,'" for those "primitive natures" whose "puerile" sense of values leads them to approach ordinary things only in terms of their "immediate utility." He was after a poetic effect—not the "false dream of the marvelous," which he thought fit only for "vulgar and common natures," but something quiet and austere. He wanted to penetrate through to "the hidden intimacy of 'ordinary things,'" which normally goes unnoticed in the everyday lifeworld of activity and striving. It was Carrà's intuition that we can only see this occulted side of things once we divorce them from their utility or instrumentality, and depict them simply and in a clearly delineated space.

Discrete Objects

Carrà's intuition is clearly embodied in his metaphysical paintings, which give evidence of a formal language and conceptual underpinning representing something analogous to what Husserl described as going back to the things themselves.

Carrà's anti-metaphysical metaphysics is epitomized by the *Natura morta con la squadra* of 1917, an undoubted masterpiece from his Ferrara period. The painting is remarkable for its formal clarity and balanced composition. Carrà depicts five simple objects: a bottle, a set-square, a jug or pitcher on a slant-topped plinth, and a strange, egg-like object with a rim or raised edge—in a kind of cube or tiny room open to view at the front. The colors are muted—grey, matte white, olive green, ochre. The objects' edges are sharply delineated, as are the shadows they throw against the walls surrounding them.

Each thing within the interior is shown as a discrete entity, as something well-defined in what it is. The set-square is plainly the object that it is, an instrument taken from a world of instrumentalities. Likewise the bottle and pitcher. As Carrà rendered them, all of these things are simple solids with plain surfaces, unitary objects that, taken individually, are like scaled-down minimalist sculptures in that they lack complex internal relationships between parts or between part and whole. They are wholes without parts. Even with its handle, the pitcher seems to have been made from a single chunk of matter; the empty space enclosed by the eye in the set-square doesn't take away from that object's integrity as a unitary thing. This strategy of taking simple forms and endowing them with solidity and volume was central to Carrà's practice at the time and was taken even further with the 1919 *Natura morta metafisica*, a painting of a room sparsely populated by the simple solids of a cylinder, a three-dimensional wedge and a cube in addition to a goblet and sculpture of a child's head.

Paintings such as the *Natura morta con la squadra* display the formal means Carrà devised for provoking the move from the mundane to the metaphysical. The well-defined, paratactical relationships he used to structure his arrangements of objects isolated them and offered them up as self-contained things divorced from any necessary relationship to each other. The *Gentiluomo ubriaco* ("drunken gentleman") of 1916 is exemplary in this regard. Set out on a surface within a darkened space are: a bottle; a striped baton; a white mask or sculpted head teetering on a cylindrical stand; a cup bisected by the right edge of the canvas. Like the objects in the *Natura morta con la squadra*, the objects here are holistically simple. Each of them holds to its own space without regard to the others; as entirely discrete entities, they have little communication with each other. Their mutual isolation is palpable, and is an essential element of the painting's composition.

If the individual objects in this and in the other paintings of 1916-1919 lack any real internal relationships, the relationships that do define them are purely external. Carrà's composition arranges them in such a way that they form a network of juxtapositions—a parataxis of adjacency without involvement. Unlike de Chirico's metaphysical interiors, which typically contain a clutter of closely massed, overlapping forms, Carrà's compositions contain objects whose surfaces and edges seem to be absolute boundaries enforcing a strict isolation. Each thing inhabits a space of its own, simply and tangibly. In effect, this isolation, simplicity and tangibility, taken together, served as the fulcrum on which Carrà's metaphysical paintings balanced.

Things Without Alibis

Everyday objects, such as those Carra painted, have a central if often unreflected-on role in the lifeworld each of us inhabits. Our existence is reflected back to us in the things that potentially play a part in that existence: as tools, obstacles, ornaments, and so forth. Human existence is to a significant extent lack; these ordinary objects are emblems of the necessary measures needed to negotiate our everyday lifeworld and its resistances, and somehow to make good that lack. But as we've seen, Carrà's formal treatment of these objects removes them from that everyday lifeworld. In effect, he displaces them. Consequently, the world Carrà's "ordinary things" inhabit is an atopia, a place where things are displaced and consequently left stranded and out of place. Getting from the everyday lifeworld to the atopia of the metaphysical interior is a matter of substituting a different perspective for the perspective of the everyday. It involves a way of seeing these things by virtue of their formal relationships rather than their given functions.

The perspective that Carrá opens up on his "ordinary things" is functionally equivalent to one that the Russian literary theorist Viktor Shklovsky termed *ostranenie*—alienation, or estrangement. As a literary device, *ostranenie* involves the wrenching of words or verbal images out of their ordinary context in order to reveal them in a new and extraordinary light. Transposed from language to painting, *ostranenie* consists in depicting ordinary things in extraordinary combinations or settings—as, for example, through the kind of parataxis and isolation Carrà used to structure his metaphysical interiors and still life paintings. With those devices Carrá created his particular sense of *ostranenie* by disrupting the relationship between the object and the everyday lifeworld—the world of action, of projects and the various pursuits of human interests and desires. He accomplished this when he freed the object from its function and submitted it to perception on the basis of its being as a brute physical fact—as mute surface, volume, and form.

That is, as a thing in all its contingent existence, in its standing out from the background of the everyday as an unjustified and possibly unjustifiable knot of matter. By making them stand out so plainly, Carrá brought his objects out into the light of the unfamiliar, throwing them into a high relief where they can't be ignored or taken for granted as instrumentalities. Rather than being shaded in the atmosphere of enigma—to use one of de Chirico's most favored terms—they are instead disclosed in their banality and existential awkwardness.

The contrast with de Chirico's metaphysical interiors, and by extension with de Chirico's concept of metaphysical painting, is illuminating. De Chirico's interiors are visual puzzles cluttered with strange or ambiguous things whose shapes obscure each other and whose identity is often indeterminate. De Chirico's collection of objects—mannequins, architect's tools, biscuits, maps or pictures on easels, partial picture frames, fish and fragments of whatever else—cluster in a knot of relationships whose meaning we can only guess at. The strangeness of it all hints at an esoteric significance derived from a personal mythology: inanimate things become oracles transmitting an all but indecipherable message. Whereas despite formal simplifications, with Carrá we always know what it is we're looking at—a set-square; a pitcher; a bottle; a cube, cylinder or wedge; a statue head. A thing standing against us in its thingness.

The message here is plain: the isolation and sheer being-there of these things bears witness to the contingency of their existence. To that extent they are things without alibis. For de Chirico's things, by contrast, their enigma is their alibi. De Chirico's metaphysical interiors are Delphic where Carrà's are atopian. That at least is the logical culmination of the estrangement he works on them, both by isolating them and by reducing their forms to a plain geometry. This simplification and isolation limit our perspective on them, but limit is the beginning of meaning: the reduced and displaced figure is, as Carrà put it in his 1918 statement "Metaphysical Painting," "an image of the form so brightly lit that it arrests reality itself."

What Carrà's best metaphysical paintings reveal, then, is that the "hidden intimacy" of things consists in their pure thingness: in the sheer accident of their existing at all. Remove its immediate utility—separate it from its readiness to submit to our use—and we are compelled to confront the object *qua* object as something existing with a mode of being of its own. Carrà may not have intended to arrange this confrontation—or at least not a confrontation with this outcome—but his depiction of the objects in his metaphysical paintings bring it about not only by isolating these things from their functions, but by thrusting them out toward us in plain sight, as so many opacities erupting into our field of vision. Strip them of their functional content in this way and they are returned to the brute fact of their particular existence. The fullness of their three-dimensionality—the volume and solidity that Carrà was concerned above all to capture, and did so successfully with his metaphysical paintings—becomes an index of their radical contingency and a visual sign of the purely accidental nature of their being here. Call it the ontological scandal of there being something rather than nothing. This is what the object in its isolation tells of itself—the gratuitousness of its existing here, now, in this form and not in another: the gratuitousness of its existing at all. It turns out that it is their radical contingency that constitutes the intimate secret of ordinary things.

On Russell Atkins' Poetics of Objectified Mind

The Ontology of the Poem-Object

The poetry of Russell Atkins may not be, as Sartre claimed of Francis Ponge's poems, on the side of objects, but rather are meant to be objects themselves. To this extent Atkins' poetry is an ontological poetry—a poetry as much about the poem's status as a kind of thing as it is about anything else. This in itself may not be remarkable or unique to Atkins—after all, any poem is an object, an artifact made of words which, once made, takes on a life independent of its creator and the fact of its creation. Thus when Atkins states, in the Preface to his 1991 collection *Juxtapositions*, that his poems are the products of his "object-forming processes at work," he may seem to be repeating a truism that holds not only for poetry but for any artwork. Consider that through the creative process the artist brings about an opening through which the object—the poem, the painting, the composition and even, arguably, the concept when a physical embodiment is lacking—comes into being, and what Atkins describes is something of a universal constant of creativity. The artist, as object-maker, is the source of the object's existence (or, to revert to the language of ontology, is the ground of the object's being). So far, a more or less conventional model of the poem-object as the product of the creative process, whatever this latter may be. Where Atkins puts his own stamp on this model is first of all in his insistence that the poem-object is the projection of a specifically internal process—what elsewhere in his Preface he calls "a kind of objectification of 'mind'"—and secondly in his assertion that the matter of the object's "relevance" or ability to communicate or to "mean"—this latter presumably in the sense of having a paraphrasable, indicative content—is simply irrelevant.

A Thing Whose Thingness Is the Material of Language

The ontological claim implied above—that Atkins' work has a certain mode of being by virtue of its having come into being in a certain way—is worth a quick detour here. It only seems fair to ask, What kind of thing is this poem-object if it comes about through the "objectification of 'mind?'" That such an objectification culminates in an object can be taken for granted, but what here could be "mind" and what would be its relationship to the resulting object? Casting "mind" in terms of intention or felt experience might get at some aspects of its role vis-à-vis the poem-object, but more fundamental is its standing as the originary event, the nexus and provocation that in two senses stands before the object it gives rise to—by virtue of being both prior to it and outside of, and other to, it as well. "Mind" as the event of the poem-object is mind as the origin or ground that leaves a trace of itself in the poem-object. Mind becomes object through an action on the part of the poet—the opening or "objectification" Atkins speaks of—and relates itself to itself through the object that it is not but that contains its trace and puts it out into the world as something independent of itself. It is itself and not itself, or rather it is itself as that image of itself that is sayable. A material expression, in other words. A kind of thing whose thingness is the material of language, a material into which the event of mind disappears. This material of the poem-object—the language out of which it is constructed—links the intangible event of mind to the physicality of the world. To the extent that the event of mind consists in the extra-linguistic, it may be that something of the event escapes language even as language shapes the expression—literally gives it form—of the event. The possibility that this is a question of fit between two different modalities—mind as such on the one hand, and language on the other—would seem to imply that the fit won't necessarily be perfect. And by extension that the possibility that at least some residue of mind will elude transposition into language cannot be discounted. But since the focus here is on the poem-object itself this question of the fit, or misfit, between mind and poem-object will have to be a question for another time. Suffice it for now to say that the poem-object is the result of a transformation and transposition—perhaps even a transubstantiation —of the event of mind into the language into which it disappears, even as it leaves traces of itself. Mind, the originary, the event, the disappearance whose material image is its trace, is memorialized in the poem-object.

A Drive Toward Exteriorization

When Atkins speaks of his poetry as consisting in an objectification of mind he is in effect asserting a claim to a poetics of expression, although "expression" is not a word he uses. He prefers the more general term "creativity" to describe his poetics. Nevertheless the process and principles he enunciates in both the Preface and *Manifesto* (this latter also included in *Juxtapositions*) make it clear that his creative ethos does assume a form of expression, albeit one with a meaning specific to him. Atkins' poetic of expression, to the extent that it involves the objectification of mind, would seem to entail the exteriorization into language of the poet's inner state, however constituted and of whatever content. Which is to say that it consists in an opening out of an internal condition or event that subsequently takes on the object existence of language. (Of course this internal event could also consist in the free play of language within the mind, in which case its taking on the object existence of language is always already accomplished.) The meaning of the poem is thus something like an image of interiority projected outward. (Granted, "interiority" is a term with a metaphysically burdened history, but as a rough metaphor for a mode of being that can only be approached metaphorically, it will have to do.) It is this objectification, or projection, that stands at the heart of Atkins' artistic practice and that grounds its meaning—this, and not any urge to communicate.

Atkins' refusal to take communication as the model or goal for poetry is a deliberate element within his poetics; he states as much when he says in the *Manifesto* that the product of artistic practice "need *not* communicate" (emphasis in the original). The stereotypical convention regarding communication—that it consists in the transmission of information about things and situations in the surrounding world, and that it can be verified or refuted by a third party on the basis of how things actually are in that world—becomes irrelevant. What is relevant is the poem-object's having been given rise to as a necessary moment of expression, which Atkins characterizes as its "drive to be brought into existence." The expressive moment just is enacted in the poem-object's drive toward exteriorization; its expression is its projection toward being and its reason for being. This reason for being need not be reduced to, or supplemented by, any communicative intention. It is that it simply is.

Idiolect and Association

It might seem that Atkins' expressionist poetic, in its refusal to communicate, would strand the poem entirely on the side of the interiority that it objectifies. If so, we would seem to be caught in a trap here—a trap of moated interiority, of a pure solipsism enclosed within itself. This would be misleading, though, even if in his *Manifesto* Atkins licenses the use of solipsism in poetry "if necessary." For it is precisely in the decision for objectification that the image of interiority runs into a reality outside of itself and molds itself through that reality—the reality of language as always already meaning-laden material. Language as external reality is language as a kind of common property, an accretion of past gestures and future possibilities existing between and transcending any specific instance of use. In being exteriorized into language, the image of interiority is permeated by an external reality characterized by conventions of usage, orthography, definition, and so on. Even when some of those conventions are defied or distorted, as for example with Atkins' well-known propensity to use an apostrophe rather than the usual "e" as the penultimate character in verbs in the past tense, they make themselves known to us surreptitiously, through the frustrated expectations that their absence or violation precipitates. Appropriated uncommonly, language conventions' commonality becomes dramatically apparent.

And yet at the same time that language is held in common by a community of users, it also reveals itself to be something different for the different members of that same community. Consider that at a coarse-grained level, different language users' understandings of a given convention or meaning held in common by the community can be expected to coincide. The finer-grained one gets in explicating a rule of usage or elucidating a meaning, though, the more and greater differences are likely to emerge between users; the more these rules' and meanings' peripheries and boundaries are likely to reveal themselves as fuzzy. (This difference between language as common property and language as appropriated by individual users corresponds, roughly, to the difference between on the one hand the structural constants of language, and on the other hand, the contingencies of language as actually internalized and used in specific situations.) In addition to what words mean—that is, the concepts and categories they embody—there is the matter of *how* they mean for any given user, which is to say the matter of the associations they carry, affective, aesthetic and otherwise, which gives them an extra-semantic or extra-grammatical resonance and which will necessarily be different for different people. Think, for example, of Rimbaud's assigning to the vowels of the alphabet specific colors and the phenomena that embody them in his sonnet *Voyelles*. This stands as an example of a systematic —or quasi-systematic—way of bringing to explicit self-awareness a set of linkages that ordinarily operate unthinkingly and on the basis of impressions formed through one's history of lived experiences. When we consider language at this level it reveals itself to be *for individual users* an idiolect whose specific meanings and internal relationships are a matter of individual peculiarities based on individual histories and experiences. One may well speak a common tongue, but with one's own accent.

As it pertains to poetry, the non-semantic, associative linkages permeating language may play a significant role. They may, for example, hold the answers to certain questions such as, Why is this word or this combination of words, or this grammatical construction, put into the poem? If not for their contribution to a referential meaning then perhaps by virtue of the associations they encode individually or in combination, possibly in their sounds or even, in the case of written poetry, their visual appearance or position on the page. All of this may be known only to the poet but that doesn't preclude these associations from contributing to—or in extreme cases entirely constituting—the poem's meaning. In fact a poem composed entirely on the basis of idiolectical chains of association may well be an example of the methodological solipsism Atkins' poetics expressly permits. There is meaning here, but it doesn't reduce to reference to an external object or situation but rather to how the words are situated within the poet's network of associations. In a sense this is the most purely expressive, and interior, kind of meaning—one that crystallizes and even dramatizes the idiolectical dimension of language Can such a meaning be communicated? Possibly not, and possibly most likely not. But this lack of communicability is no drawback for a poetry like Atkins,' which isn't necessarily grounded in a communicative intent anyway.

Atkins' poetic seems to demonstrate an intuitive grasp of language as it functions at this level of individual engagement. Consider that with the objectification of the image of interiority there is involved a complex, reciprocal movement: language imposes itself as an exterior material through which the image of interiority must be expressed, but at the same time the image of interiority appropriates language precisely on the basis of the idiolectical networks of affective, aesthetic and other associations that permeate language as the language user knows it. Interiority imposes its own idiolectical nuances on the external material of language, in other words. It may be with something like a sense of language-as-idiolect in mind that Atkins, in his *Manifesto*, asserts that one should "question 'the language of common speech'...[and] let poetry thrust toward a language 'peculiar to itself.'" Exactly how it might do that is a subject Atkins addresses in his *Manifesto*.

Foregrounding the Aesthetic

The basic principle animating Atkins' poetics of expression, and hence his methodology, is as fundamental as it is categorical: the poet is the ground of being for the poem-object. As he puts it in the *Manifesto*, the poet must "be the source of everything" and consequently will set the conditions for the bringing-into-existence of the poem-object. Everything that conditions the poem-object comes from the poet, who should not "risk these conditions for what is called 'communication.'" Clarity of reference or "sense," as embodied in the plain voice conveying precisely or economically some item of information, should accordingly be avoided if it risks compromising the expressive force or experimental makeup of the work. Or, as Atkins puts it, "do not destroy a poem trying to make it clear." In his own poetry, Atkins puts this tenet into practice by pushing to the fore those aspects of the poem that are salient not on the basis of their semantic sense but by virtue of their aesthetic sense.

In order to do this, Atkins advocates techniques or methods geared toward foregrounding the aesthetic or connotative aspects of the poem through a special handling of language. He recommends, for example, that the poet make his or her technique "explicit." Specific ways of doing this might include using unconventional, non-everyday language rhythms or constructing the poem in a way that will block the reader's ability to bypass or penetrate the poem's aesthetic-connotative qualities to get right to the denotative "sense," if any. One method he recommends for deflecting the search for sense involves a kind of referential conflation through word substitution, in which the poet exploits words' potential to signify multiple meanings. In concrete terms, using different words to say the same thing—or conversely, using the same words to say different things—by for example repeating or reusing previously used words in different contexts. Beyond the fact that many words do by definition convey multiple meanings, this technique potentially provides an opening in which the idiolectical dimension of language may play a significant role in the poem's composition. For, if the poet were to put Atkins' advice into practice he or she might make word choices by distinguishing relationships of similarity and difference not by virtue of reference or dictionary definitions alone, but also—or instead—on the basis of the extra-referential associations words carry within his or her idiolect. (We could even define an idiolect as in part consisting in a differential system based on contrasts of associations—affective, aesthetic, experiential and otherwise extra-referential—specific to the language user, as well as of conventional, interpersonally accessible meanings.)

In fact selecting diction on the basis of idiolectical associations rather than dictionary definitions, even in cases where the latter allows multiple meanings to the same word, would be a highly effective way of constituting a poem as a network of significations opaque to any attempt to be deciphered as a plainly referring object. Atkins seems to get at this dimension of linguistic meaning when he says to:

> Make use of "implicitness" since a poem is not obligated to avoid inherent meaning similarities...Most grass may be "green" but the word "green" has its own properties.

Not only that, but the properties "green" has can be expected to vary from person to person. My concept of "green" may not be your concept of "green," hence the word "green" will call up different mental images—perhaps in the form of different shades of green, or different objects that epitomize what "green" is or what it should look like. Through these conceptual and perhaps other kinds of linkages words do have their own properties, and some of these properties, over and above (or "implicit" and below) their commonly held, conventionally defined meanings, are peculiar to the individual language user. If Atkins' encouragement to the poet to be solipsistic is to draw its force as a practical compositional strategy we could expect to find it here, in the principle that idiolectical associations provide a legitimate ground on which to base a poetics.

Grammar, in the guise of a twisting or alienation of standard grammatical usage, has a role to play here as well. Recall Atkins' signature gesture of substituting an apostrophe for the omitted "e" before the "d" at the end of a past-tense verb. His reason for doing it, as he explains in the Preface, is to produce a "bold distortion of the weak verb" in order to conflate its functions as adjective and verb. The ambiguity Atkins hopes to create with this simultaneity of function represents a way of using a single word to suggest a branching of grammatical identities and hence to make its direction of reference uncertain. We may not be able to determine easily or even at all what noun the verb/adjective applies to, or whether it applies to any noun present in the text at all.

With the possibility of clear referential interpretation blocked, we are offered instead other interpretive possibilities, some of which are driven by aesthetic considerations in which, for example, the word's rhythm or sound, or appearance on the page, eclipses its semantic sense.

(It might be argued that the deliberate archaism of the elided "e" makes little practical difference here, and that it is instead the shape and makeup of the line or the phrase that does the actual work of confounding interpretation. While there is some merit to this observation, it would seem that Atkins' unconventional orthographic choice serves to direct attention to the word and to single it out as an interpretive fulcrum on which something of significance balances. Seeing it, the question naturally arises: Why put *this* archaism *here*, if not for a reason?)

Disclosing a World

Although in the very first item in his *Manifesto* Atkins asserts that the artwork "need *not* communicate," his poem-objects, simply by virtue of being poem-objects in the first place, do in fact engage the reader in a variety of communication. An artwork *qua* object is not just any kind of object in a world of objects but is rather a particularly meaningful kind of object. As Gianni Vattimo put it in *Art's Claim to Truth*, "the encounter with works of art is never the encounter with another thing in the world; what one encounters is another perspective on the world entering into dialogue with our own" (p. 99). We simply expect to find meaning there. This seems especially true of Atkins' poetry when considered as a poetry of expression in the sense defined above.

In exteriorizing the artist's interiority (or, in Atkins' own formulation, "the objectification of 'mind'"), the poem by its very nature discloses the artist's engagement with, or attunement to, the world. Such a disclosing object cannot help but be meaningful. The fact that it was created in the first place is an index of its meaningfulness for the artist; that it exists at all as an art object is de facto evidence of the felt necessity that brought it into existence—what Atkins calls "its drive to *be*"–in such a way that its position cannot be one of indifference, or meaninglessness.

Nor can its reception be a matter of indifference. Anyone confronting the art object must come to it with the preunderstanding that it does have meaning, that it does communicate something of the artist's being in the world, whether or not that meaning can be ascertained easily or even at all. The object is an opening through which the person seeing, hearing, or otherwise coming to it through his or her own way of being can have a meaningful experience of the artist's way of being. In short Atkins' poem-objects, by virtue of their having been created, would seem to offer what Vattimo calls a "radically new disclosure on the world." Atkins may not intend them to communicate necessarily but they nevertheless disclose; they disclose a world of meaningful engagement that constitutes a perspective. They may do so if not through their semantic content, or at least not primarily through their semantic content, then through something else—something as seemingly elusive, yet as fully encompassing and signifying, as the *Stimmung* or atmosphere they create, through aesthetic means.

Reading Russell Atkins' Exteriors, Interiors

Stimmung as Meaning

By his own assertion, Russell Atkins' poem-objects are not themselves necessarily intended to communicate, at least not in the ordinary sense of imparting information separable from the language with which that information is communicated. But lack of communicative intent does not—and cannot—equate to lack of meaning. Meaning of some order is inevitable; once brought into existence these poem-objects find themselves not only situated within a world of meanings, but made of a material—language—that itself is inherently meaningful. The poem-object simply is meaningful on grounds other than those presupposed by the existence and sharing of indicative content. For Atkins, those grounds are aesthetic.

That Atkins intends his poetry to operate—to "mean"—aesthetically rather than discursively, with a language he calls "peculiar to itself" rather than with the plain, message-transmitting "language of common speech" is explicitly set out in his *Manifesto*, from which these quotes are taken. As he also declares there the aim of poetry and of art more generally is "largely AESTHETIC, not essentially information." Paraphrasable content, to the extent that it exists, is not coextensive with poetic meaning; for the latter we need to look elsewhere. While this basic idea may be more-or-less a commonplace, the way that Atkins goes about embedding aesthetic meaning in language is his own. His poems often contain formal devices that separate them from ordinary language usages—for example, orthographic or grammatical displacements as well as unconventional arrangements of words on the page.

But there is also something else, something more pervasive that emerges from the poem as a whole—as an integral object, we could say —and to which these different poetic devices may sum. That something is the atmosphere, or *Stimmung*, that the poem creates. *Stimmung* is a meaning, but not something intended to be transparently communicated as would, say, a statement in plain language; it may be, on the contrary, the product of language used specifically to avoid the plain statement and direct transmission of information. Looking beyond the specific case of poetry, we can say that as a general matter an artwork's *Stimmung*, making itself felt through a complex of suggestion, indirection, oblique allusion, and associations made possible by the language or other material out of which it is made, creates a sense of mood and bypasses the plain communication of the purely indicative. Simply put, the work's *Stimmung* is an event arising from the ascendancy of connotation over denotation. Any aesthetic object is liable to throw off a *Stimmung* simply by virtue of being an aesthetic object; how Atkins does it is a function of the idiosyncratic way he appropriates—and more importantly, disrupts—the linguistic medium.

The Seer

The poem "Exteriors, Interiors" from *Juxtapositions*, gives condensed expression to an expansive atmospheric effect. The poem was inspired by the painting *The Seer* by Giorgio de Chirico; the poem itself seems not to be an ekphrasis or direct interpretation of the painting but rather a creative projection taking the shape of an imaginative scenario provoked by the painting. Not an appendage or an afterthought to *The Seer* but rather a counterpart to it—a complementary yet autonomous object bound to the painting through an affinity of affect.

De Chirico himself was a painter for whom *Stimmung* was a supreme artistic value, particularly for the paintings of his metaphysical period, during which *The Seer* was created. Painted during de Chirico's time in Paris just before the First World War the picture, like several other of de Chirico's paintings from that period, depicts a mannequin—the seer of the title—in an ambiguous setting seemingly neither wholly indoors nor outdoors. Situated in front of the mannequin is a blackboard; on it are sketched in outline some of the objects from the iconography that appeared in de Chirico's earlier metaphysical paintings. These objects, in a sense familiars of de Chirico's, include an arcade, a statue seen from the back, a wall. In the background is a strange building with classical elements: a pair of Doric columns against a blind wall flanked on either side by an arch. Beside the arch to the right is a drawn curtain similar to the one that appears in *The Enigma of the Oracle*. Jutting out from the painting's right edge is the shadow of what might be a statue on a plinth. Like de Chirico's other exterior/interior paintings of the time, it shows a static scene. The moment it captures is immobile. A terminal stillness permeates this strange habitation of inanimate objects. What then does Atkins make of this, or rather, make out of it?

A Pervasive Uncertainty

Whether intended or not, the poem's title—*Exteriors, Interiors*—is an indication of what is going on within it. Atkins takes the exteriority of the scene depicted in de Chirico's painting and transposes it to the interiority of the poem's speaker—to the speaker's way of grasping himself within that scene. The scene permeates the speaker's state of mind; the speaker's state of mind permeates the scene: all of this crystallizes in the *Stimmung* of the poem, which in turn is elucidated in Atkins' dislocations of diction and grammar.

At the outset, Atkins obliquely introduces a scene of quiet and solitude—of "this place that wishes to be left/to its own devices" which is "awhiled with wan, long-length'd." This is no description of a location in terms of its observable qualities alone—of the qualities one sees, but rather of the qualities one sees in it or, better yet, sees into it. We get an indication of this in Atkins' strange construction "awhiled," which together with "long-length'd" connotes a place extended in time or through time as experienced qualitatively by the speaker, rather than a place measured in physical distance. It is a place where a "long-length'd" period of time has gone by, perhaps as represented by the lengthening shadows so often encountered in de Chirico's metaphysical exteriors and encountered in *The Seer* in the shadow projecting in from the picture's right edge. The speaker has been here a while, long enough to experience the shadows creeping slowly at a feeble, "wan" pace. This is a place, in sum, of affective engagement, where length is measured in the subjective sense of time's passage, of its moving weakly. And yet somewhat ominously as well. For the speaker, this place is shot through "with the solemnity of loomed/ footfall'd." The strangeness of this characterization, which implies much but divulges little, is codified by the linguistic structure Atkins uses—one which ends abruptly with "footfall'd," a dangling construction apparently of Atkins' invention and certainly of his mannered spelling. It is an odd coinage that, like "loomed" just before it, seems to function as an adjective but which has no noun attached to it. The absence of a noun here creates the sense of something hidden, something hinted at but not there. The missing noun is a trace, but a trace of what? It is only at the end of the poem that the non-presence the absent noun reveals in its absence will present itself.

The second stanza brings in the speaker, who appears to be an observer of the scene and of the something there that seems not to be there. He is present to a presence that remains out of view—"the one/ out and out/who is *not* seen"—and yet is felt just beyond the edge of what can be physically perceived. It's a strange mode of being—a presence ostensibly poised in the exteriority of the surrounding scene yet known only through its position within the interiority of the speaker's affective state. In addition, this strangely liminal presence—perhaps because it is liminal, because it is felt and not seen—provokes a mood of self-doubt within the speaker. It is a mood that Atkins emphasizes by using, three times, the word "certain"—as a kind of thesis ("I'm certain"), answered by an opposing antithesis ("not being certain") that leaves the speaker with a non-synthesis suspended within a counterfactual:

> ...If I could enter now
> behind the arch, for example
>   (the where
> the one watches) I feel as certain as I am
> leaning...

(Even the basic device of lineation takes on aesthetic import and contributes to the *Stimmung* of uncertainty. Here and throughout the poem the lines stagger down the page in a seemingly arbitrary manner, suggesting the footfalls of someone on an uncertain footing.)

Atkins' construction "the where" here is anomalous—an apparent case of elision in which a noun phrase is missing its noun. One would normally expect to find a word like "place" between "the" and "where" here, but like the presence the speaker feels, its appearance is as a non-appearance. It is another absence that serves to contribute to the overall mood of uncertainty. Where we would expect to find the word "place" (or something similar to it) we only find "where," which in the absence of a concrete indication of place seems to become the unanswered question—"where?"

The fact of place itself is displaced here, removed or never there, an exterior rendered *atopos* rendered—strange, out of place—through the speaker's interior transformation. If "long-length'd" refers at least in part to the shadow cutting across the scene it is applicable not just to a literal shadow thrown off by an object blocking the light but to the shadow of doubt that seems to enfold the speaker.

And Yet a Paradoxical Certainty

As noted above, it is only at the end of the poem that Atkins gives thematic, if not grammatical, closure to the dangling construction "footfall'd." We learn that it is the "one who is *not* seen/who/footfalls." This someone unseen may be someone only imagined, someone non-existent in fact—no more substantial than the creeping, long shadow by which the speaker's sense of time is measured. As with many of de Chirico's metaphysical paintings, Atkins' poem implies a presence that makes itself known only indirectly, through oblique clues and traces, which here seem to take the form of the sound of footsteps. And also as with de Chirico's paintings the presence's apparently not being there is an index of its in fact being there; the footfalls the speaker hears, or imagines hearing, are pure contingencies, possibilities made possible by the transposition to an interior key of the enigmatic world de Chirico painted—a world in which non-being, in the guise of the flux of becoming, is Being's most convincing alibi. It is a necessarily ambiguous alibi, though, precisely to the extent that it is grounded in the possibility of the non-being of Being. Confronted with it, one is always and inevitably "certain of not being certain/that there is someone" there. That there is anything there, or that anything was there or could be there at all. It is this paradoxical certainty grounded in uncertainty that Atkins' *Exteriors, Interiors* communicates—perhaps unintentionally, but nevertheless it does communicate--by aesthetic and non-indicative means. Through the *Stimmung* it discloses.

The Enigma of the Hour

It may be a train station, or one of the arcaded buildings common in Turin and other Italian cities. A two-story construction with arches on the ground level, rectangular windows at the second level and a tiled roof, it sits at the center of the picture plane, continuing beyond both edges. An open, public space—a piazza of some sort—opens out in front of the building.

Oddly, the building and piazza feel as if they ought to be deserted, but they aren't. There are three human figures coexisting here—coexisting, but effectively isolated from each other. One, wrapped in white and facing away from the viewer, is in the foreground by a pool with a small fountain; a second huddles in shadow in the shallow space of the building's interior; the third is barely visible at a second-story window just to the left of a clock. The building and its surrounding space are sunk in shadow at the moment—a moment that could be situated at the beginning or end of the day.

In either case, what we see is the visual evidence of a disorienting hour when objects and people take on a grey, soft-edged appearance, and distances are difficult to judge. The ambiguity of the time of day is cleared up by the clock above the arches, which signals five minutes before three. Presumably this is mid-afternoon in late autumn or winter, when the daylight wanes early. Although the hour of Giorgio de Chirico's great painting *The Enigma of the Hour* (1910-1911*) can reasonably be disambiguated, the unsettling character—the enigma—of the picture remains.

"Enigma" is the keyword of the painting's title. Starting with *The Enigma of an Autumn Afternoon* and the slightly earlier *The Enigma of the Oracle*, which may have been titled retroactively, the word turns up in a number of the paintings de Chirico produced during his metaphysical period, which ran from 1909 to 1919. The word and the concept it represented, which de Chirico understood in a specific and idiomatic way, provided the foundation for the painter's aesthetic during this period.

De Chirico claimed to have discovered enigma in Florence in 1909. While there, he had an epiphany that proved to be a turning point in his development as an artist. As he described it in an early, handwritten text, he was sitting in the Piazza Santa Croce after recuperating from an illness, and consequently was in "a nearly morbid state of sensitivity." He suddenly felt he was seeing his surroundings for the first time, seeing through their ordinary appearances, in a sense. He described this moment of revelation as "an enigma;" the concept became central to his art and turns up frequently in the various manuscript texts written between 1911 and 1913 in which de Chirico formulated his early aesthetic philosophy.

The Enigma of an Autumn Afternoon was the concrete product of the Piazza Santa Croce revelation and signaled the beginning of a particularly creative period for de Chirico. The feeling it gave rise to formed the basis for a series of subsequent paintings, including *The Enigma of the Hour*. For de Chirico the enigma consisted not only in the revelation of the world around him, but, as he wrote in "Meditations of a Painter," he also "liked to call the resulting work an enigma." The artwork was an enigma to the extent that it was "a *thing* that produces a sensation" by refusing the temptation to take the world as it presents itself to us in its ordinary guise. De Chirico called this a Nietzschean aesthetic, but it also reflects the deep influence that the philosophy of Schopenhauer had on him. In explicating his notion of the enigma he turned to a passage from Schopenhauer's *Parerga und Paralipomena* which asserts that in order to disclose the true nature of things, "it is enough to isolate oneself so absolutely from the world and things for a few moments that the most ordinary objects and events appear completely new and unknown." This is precisely a description of what de Chirico felt had happened to him in the Piazza Santa Croce. Consistent with Schopenhauer's pronouncement, de Chirico's experience in Florence revealed the world of the everyday as something alien and uncanny in which one no longer feels at home. This moment of revelation is an enigma to the extent that it throws new light onto ordinary things, disclosing them as something unexpected and extraordinary. As interpreted in the metaphysical paintings, the light it throws on them is—quite literally—the light of twilight.

The Meaning of the Shadow

Like many of the metaphysical paintings, *The Enigma of the Hour* is pervaded by an atmosphere of crepuscularity. The quality of light and the muted colors suggest a sun close to the horizon; the scene is twilit and dominated by shadow. For de Chirico, twilight carried a significant expressive weight. Twilight is an inherently ambiguous state —a period of transition common to both nightfall and daybreak. On the evidence of the hour marked out on the clock *The Enigma of the Hour* seems to depict an autumn sunset; many of the other metaphysical paintings set outdoors depict dawns—a time that de Chirico declared to be "the hour of enigma." For most of these paintings, though, engulfing shadows are central motifs.

For de Chirico, the shadow was a kind of index of enigma. As he put it in one of the manuscripts, "there is more of enigma in the shadow of a man walking in the sun than in all the religions of the past, present and future." It's little wonder that he connected a shadow-engulfed world to enigma. By its nature, shadow is a multivalent carrier of meaning. Correlated as it is with the movement of the sun, the shadow is a natural sign indicating the time of day. That would seem to be simple enough. But beyond its natural meaning it carries a meaning liable to interpretation in terms of human rhythms and projects. A long shadow signals time getting short to complete something, night approaching and time to turn homeward, a downshifting of activity and an impending move to a resting state. Or it can signal the transition of night to day, that moment just before the time one emerges from oneself and into the world outside to begin work or otherwise to engage in public life. With its relatively low stimulus environment and implicit promise of concealment, twilight is conducive to reflection or introspection, creating the kind of otherworldly atmosphere in which enigma, as de Chirico understood it, could make itself felt.

Thus de Chirico's depiction of shadow does more than record a particular moment of the day during a particular season; instead, it serves to create a pervasive atmosphere or *Stimmung*—the German word he favored in the early manuscripts to describe the mood of an artwork. Atmosphere was for de Chirico a substantial presence that could realize the potential of things to convey meaning; in his "Meditations of a Painter," he could well have been describing the twilit *Stimmung* of *The Enigma of the Hour* when he described a moment when "the light and shadows, the lines, the angles, all the mysteries of volume begin to speak." It is through this crepuscular atmosphere, emblematized by the shadow, that de Chirico's metaphysical paintings suggest something deeply felt about being in time, through time.

Time and Transience

Being in time is a particular mode of being peculiar to humans. In an important sense, time comes into the world through human self-consciousness. In one sense, time exists as a humanly-instituted, quantitative measure of change. Beyond time as a quantitative construct, there is a sense of time as meaningful, as carrying a significance that only we, as finite, futurally-oriented self-conscious beings, disclose. The experience of human temporality is the experience of being finite and relentlessly projecting into a future that must at some point run up against the limit of nonexistence. It is precisely this finitude and intimation of limit that gives time its human meaning.

As such, human temporality is susceptible to the sense of unsettledness or disquiet that arises in the face of the uncertainty of the future. It may be a matter of a choice I have to make or something I have to do, the outcome of which is never guaranteed. Our constantly projecting into the future orients us toward something only vaguely known or unknown that hasn't yet confronted us. We live in time through a kind of anxiety coming to us from the future, as it were. But there is another disquieting experience of time that points in the other direction—toward the past. This is the experience of transience or impermanence. It is the experience of time that, embodied in the mood of crepuscularity, permeates *The Enigma of the Hour*.

Through the sense of transience we apprehend the world as being-in-flux, as a process of becoming and, more importantly, becoming nonexistent. The Presocratic philosopher Heraclitus was one of the earliest and most evocative thinkers to put the notion of flux at the center of his philosophy; he encapsulated it in the saying, quoted in Plato's *Cratylus*, that "all beings move and nothing remains still." Appropriately enough, Heraclitus was the third philosopher—beside Schopenhauer and Nietzsche—whose ideas played a significant role in forming de Chirico's metaphysical aesthetic. The focal figure of *The Enigma of the Oracle*, a pensive figure wrapped in a dark cloak facing away from the viewer, may in fact be meant to represent the Greek Ionian philosopher—"the Ephesian meditating in the faint light of dawn," as de Chirico imagined him in a typically evocative early text.

(Iconographically, the figure itself traces back to Böcklin's painting of Odysseus and Calypso, but in appropriating it for his own use de Chirico may well have intended it to represent the philosopher.) In *The Enigma of the Hour* an echo of this figure appears twice, first in white in the foreground by the fountain, and secondly and more obscurely as a dark shape in the window to the left of the clock. But whether or not Heraclitus is supposed to be symbolized by these figures, he does seem to preside over the picture's engagement of time and loss. Its engagement with being-in-flux.

Nostalgia and Lost Time

The awareness of being-in-flux is the awareness that the world is something temporary—a passing configuration of objects, events and states of affairs in which things that appear solid eventually erode and vanish, and become lost in time. This consciousness of loss brings with it a sense of being as an ongoing process of dispossession, of the separation of oneself from oneself and one's world by the action of time. If time is the engine of dispossession then the awareness of transience is the awareness that discloses time as the engine of *our* dispossession. In effect, the world that being-in-flux discloses as temporary is our world; it brings time down from the level of abstraction to the lived world of the concrete.

Ultimately, the experience of being-in-flux and the correlated awareness of the transience of oneself and one's world is the experience of a particular kind of negation. For, like the future, the past represents a negation of the present, albeit in its own particular way. If the future negates the present in the name of a posited situation that doesn't yet exist, the past negates the present through the non-presence of the people and things that are no longer there. It is a kind of nothingness secreted in the heart of the present.

The nothingness that the past represents is a paradoxical one, though, in that it leaves behind monuments and traces inscribed in the material world of the present. De Chirico's metaphysical paintings reveled in this paradox, with their portrayals of the piazzas, towers and arcades that stood as landmarks in a twilit world—as monuments to lost time as memorialized in the stolidity of architecture.

The awareness of lost time is the defining theme in many of de Chirico's paintings of the metaphysical period. It often took the form of an explicit invocation of nostalgia and melancholy—two words that appear repeatedly in the titles of the metaphysical paintings as well as in his literary work. Both melancholy and nostalgia are moods that are themselves transient, but as such they are symptoms of a deeper grasp of time as dispossessor of being and of the past as a nothingness that nevertheless is palpable. The crepuscular world these paintings portray is a world pervaded by nostalgia—a world we regretfully apprehend as withdrawing from us in time.

(Interestingly, the mood of nostalgia and lost time that permeates the metaphysical paintings doesn't entirely vanish after de Chirico's turn toward classicism. In effect, it permeates and defines the larger project that the neoclassical paintings were a later part of. Nostalgia and the sense of lost time were the outward manifestation of the sensibility that makes of de Chirico's work a unified whole, despite the stylistic shifts it underwent over the years.)

Enigma and Finitude

Ultimately, the enigma of things consists in their transience. This seems to be the fundamental psychological insight communicated through the metaphysical paintings, which portray nothing if not a world apprehended as being-in-flux. But gleaning this from the paintings entails recognizing the impossibility of one of de Chirico's methodological ideals and rejecting the metaphysics behind the metaphysical paintings, as it were.

Under the influence of Schopenhauer's distinction between the phenomenal world and the reality underlying it, de Chirico declared that to grasp and to portray the enigma of things was "to suppress the human as a point of reference." But if time is the key to the enigma, this suppression cannot be effected. The world as such isn't in time the way we are—time is something that happens to things, to objects, whereas time is something that we experience and make sense of. We can imagine the things inhabiting de Chirico's metaphysical paintings—the fountains, architecture and even the human figures—as enigmatic because of our way of being in time. It is through our self-awareness as finite beings that we grasp these things as transient and disclose them in the crepuscular mood that de Chirico so powerfully conveyed in *The Enigma of the Hour* and many other paintings. We lend them our knowledge of our own transience, in a sense; time is disclosed as the engine of loss only for a finite being aware of its finitude.

Sticks & Stones in the Time of Objects

One sometimes hears of artists whose depictions of things, visually or verbally, penetrate to their supposed inner lives and capture the imagined psychology of these inanimate objects. As if the surfaces weren't enough or were somehow defective or otherwise an embarrassment of inarticulate immobility. But to a significant extent things—natural things, things as they are before we integrate them into our practical, affective or aesthetic lives—are their surfaces.

In his drawings and paintings of sticks and stones, Brian Olewnick intuits the depth that resides on the surfaces of these natural objects.

Portraits of Things as They Are for Themselves

An image that recurs is of a stone, vaguely ovoid in shape. Its contours are softly rounded, its topography consists of gently undulating swells and niches hinted at by impastoed paint or a contrast of color. Its size is difficult to determine, as it is portrayed by itself in an otherwise empty, circumscribed space. There is nothing to compare it to, nothing to establish its scale. It stands at the center, pushing up against the borders of the picture plane. The relationship of its mass to the surrounding space is negated *qua* relationship; its mass seems to absorb space, drawing it in and extinguishing it as an independent variable. There is the stone, its edge, and then nothing: a portrait of the thing as it is for itself.

Like Giorgio Morandi, who repeatedly painted arrangements of the same closed set of objects—bottles, jars, pitchers, and other ostensibly mundane items—Olewnick often selects his subjects from a closed universe of things. For example, the same stone appears and reappears, seen from the same, flat-on perspective. Olewnick notes his tendency to "work small, often using the same objects I've kept around and grown attached to for decades." Such a long-term acquaintance would seem to foster a capacity for surprise and a way for vision to renew itself rather than to succumb to a numbing familiarity. For all the invariance of perspective, Olewnick reveals different facets of the stone's surface through subtle changes in color and shading. Again like Morandi, he seems to show us different sides of the same object by showing us the same side in what I'm tempted to think of as its different moods.

These depictions of sticks and stones are portraits of things as we imagine they look when we aren't there to see them: mute, full, impervious to the concerns and praxes that fall outside of them even when they are made use of. For this reason we can distinguish these paintings and drawings from still lives. The organization of the still life shows the trace of the human hand which arranges things, creates a synthetic space of inanimate objects externally related to each other by virtue of that hand. And then absents itself. But its trace is still there, in the facts of abutment, adjacency, grouping and so forth—in short, in the frozen dynamic of a space organized from outside. In these images, by contrast, the hand never appears to have been there; the objects in question are juxtaposed rather than organized per se.

Consider *Two Pines*, a sketch of two pine trunks. Two thin pine trunks, drawn in a closely observed, realistic manner, float juxtaposed in an undefined, neutral space. The apparent disconnection between the two trunks reflects a deliberate pictorial decision on the part of the artist: the drawing is one of a 2009 series in which Olewnick explored his interest in portraying what he described as "two discrete objects…

in separate but shared space." In this context of seeming non-context, each is the only point of reference of the other.

These trunks aren't depicted as they would be in nature—there's no surrounding forest, buildings, field, or any other natural or artificial landmarks in relation to them—but instead are excerpted from nature, which is to say abstracted from the forest or treeline in which they were situated and then held up to view.

Paradoxically, although the two tree trunks have been isolated as objects to be viewed, their depiction effaces the trace of the eye that selected them and the hand that drew them. They appear simply as objects, adjacent to each other but otherwise not connected or brought into any relationship beyond adjacency. It's in the way that they've been drawn. They are just two pine trunks, and nothing more.

In this matter-of-fact depiction of the two trunks there would seem to be no unseen third—no observer to discover and unify the trunks into a synthetic field made whole by the observer's presence and the act of observation. Observation is the in-relation-to on the basis of which such a synthesis could be effected—a purpose transcending the brute facts of the objects present and uniting them in a field defined by that purpose.

In sum, these sticks and stones, bluntly thrusting themselves into our field of vision, seem to exist in a state that predates our having imposed an order on them. In seeing them this way we seem to move backward from the phenomenon—the thing as it appears to us—to something prior to that. Call it whatever remainder is left over once the phenomenal is subtracted. Once we are subtracted.

We may think that things are a kind of Potemkin village of dubious substance, withdrawing from us once we turn away from them. But this is to negate them needlessly. If we are somehow to encounter them in their inertia, in their thick atemporality we first must go beyond them—imagine them as something else, to grasp them as equipment, ornament or obstacle, or to read them as signs, as I believe we do here. Signs of our absence.

Paradoxically, this seeming encounter with the thing as it exists for itself comes to us by virtue of a representation of the thing—an artifact made of an appearance. I suppose this is an acknowledgement of the phenomenal as a closed loop more than anything else, and conversely as a concession to a way of being that, while foreign to us, surrounds us and yet must be approached through a kind of negation—negation of the brute fact through the imagination. Which in essence is what these, or any other representations of the mute natural thing, must be. Thus these paintings create an illusion, the illusion of an encounter with Being in its mute fullness.

The Time of Objects

The Being of a stone is atemporal. How can this be? We see this same stone, softly contoured, its shape quite clearly rounded by the effects of erosion. The stone's surface shows the effects of time. But for the stone, the future comes to it from outside; its relationship to time is a purely external one.

Time etches itself across the face of the stone with a slow hand. The smooth surfaces give evidence of the resistance of the elements to the stone's inert material. And here there is an irony: this ordinarily immobile object is worn to an aerodynamically efficient shape conducive to swift motion.

The objects we find in the natural world—sticks, stones and the like —are a plenitude because they lack nothing. Because they lack nothing they are atemporal—they don't project themselves into a future in which they make good on something they lack. They are all presence, all in the present to that extent. They are nonetheless subject to time—

they undergo erosion, decay and dissolution—but time comes to them, they do not bring time into the world by projecting a future for themselves.

Without an open future, in a sense everything is already decided. For these sticks and stones and other objects like them. True, one doesn't know exactly where or how the stone will end up—washed into a gully by a downpour, skipped over the surface of a pond by a curious or bored child, picked up and added to a collection of other stones in an artist's studio. But in all of these instances everything is decided for the stone, and here the passive voice is entirely appropriate for describing the situation of an object for which its future comes to it from outside.

Because objects' temporality is external to them—is something that acts upon them—we describe that too in the passive voice. The effects of time *are etched* across their surfaces; they *are subject* to temporality as reflected in their slow decomposition. Time is something that happens to them. Inevitably when we speak of them we speak for them, and drawing here counts as a form of speaking. In speaking for these things, as the title of one of Francis Ponge's books would have it, we take the side of objects.

Physical Counterpoint: Reflections on Sound & Movement in Duet

The arts aspire, if not to complement each other, at least to lend one another new energies. Charles Baudelaire

One of the more fruitful areas of improvisational exploration lies at the intersection of music and dance. These two very different artistic media—the one concerned with physical movement in space, and the other with sonic movement in time—relate to each other in ways that transcend the conventions of each while at the same time conserving and converting each into a language legible by the other. We can trace some of the complexities of this mutually constitutive relationship through the roles played by line and mass in the meeting of sound and movement—in a duet.

Because it reduces the music and dance partnership to its absolute minimum, the duet illustrates most clearly the dynamic within each and between both. When the interaction of music and dance is reduced to one participant from each side, each is thrown back onto his or her own resources as mediated by the other and by the other alone, in a particularly intimate kind of counterpoint. Unless the two participants choose the course of running parallel to each other with no points of contact—certainly a legitimate strategy, as Cage's work with the Cunningham group demonstrated—each will have to shape his or her part in attunement with the other, necessarily reaching across to what is specific to the other's discipline in the process.

In a performance in May of 2015 I played double bass in a mostly improvised duet with dancer Ken Manheimer. The piece, which Ken composed, was structured as a brief solo for one of us—which one of us it would be was to be decided by silent mutual consent *ad lib.* at the moment of performance—followed by an equally brief solo for the other, followed by an improvisation for both together. Although possibly not planned that way, the solo-solo-duet structure of the piece helped to establish a strong sense of linear counterpoint between us. In its most basic sense, counterpoint calls for each part or participant to play a line independent of but related to that of the other; by starting as a solo, each of us could lay the foundation for his own independent line, to be continued in relation to the other's line once the duet got underway. This laid the groundwork for what I believe was an essentially linear relationship between our parts, one expressed in a complementarity of phrasing. Silences—or pauses, more generally—played a significant role in the crafting of individual phrases and in setting up points of intersection and divergence between them. Because the performance took place on an open stage in an essentially empty surrounding space, our individual lines had no point of reference but each other.

The approach Ken and I arrived at more or less spontaneously is of course not the only one possible. An excerpt of a duet by double bassist Adriano Orrù and dancer Enrica Spada, performed in Cagliari ,in June of 2015, exemplifies a different variation on the theme of counterpointing sound and movement. Rather than being rooted in an interlinear relationship, as was my duet with Ken, this one appears to be based on a relationship of field to line. The bass sets out a kind of ground drawing on harmonics, deeply bowed open strings, spiccato bowing and other figures that form a field within which Spada's movement is set. Spada's line is marked with a clarity partly defined by the act of descending stairs, which she accomplishes with great attention paid to the play of parallels and perpendiculars as delineated by her legs, arms and torso. This play of line and angle occurs over the foundation provided by Orrù's sound, which serves as a virtual plane across which the movement takes place.

The Hybrid Line

Both of the performances described above turn on an expansive, multi-modal counterpoint. In a musical duet of any kind, counterpoint is a ready to hand, basic formal strategy. Two instruments can be brought into relationship with each other through the weaving of two independent, complementary lines running parallel or counter to each other. But as the above performances show, a musical instrument playing a line in counterpoint to movement is a different thing from counterpointing another instrument. Improvisation now takes place across artistic media or, to put it more generally, modalities of expressive action. The notion of line expands beyond the domain of the melodic or rhythmic line to encompass any sequence of pitches, sounds, gestures, and rests, each with its given duration in time or extension in space. The line in effect is a cross-modal hybrid incorporating sound, silence, physical movement, and non-movement. When this cross-modal hybrid emerges, the formal components involved in one modality reach out beyond themselves to make contact with the formal components of the other.

Consider the role of the rest in phrasing. When improvising counterpoint with another musician, one player will often read the rests marking the other's phrases—the lacunae opening up in the sequence of notes through which the phrase unfolds—as silences to be filled in order to complete the phrase or to complement it through the development of an independent yet related phrase. As a formal quality, silence is essentially temporal, a gap in the flow of time as the latter is embodied in a sequence of sounds. But when counterpoint takes place between sound and movement, the lacunae opening up in the musical phrase are read not simply as silences soliciting sound but rather as openings to action. It is precisely by reaching out across modalities—from sound to physical movement—that silences lose their character as exclusively—or even predominantly—concerned with sound and instead take on the more general nature of stillness. Even while remaining quantitatively constant, they undergo a qualitative change.

Texture (from Surface to Mass)

If the horizontal dimension of counterpoint is to be found in the line, the vertical dimension consists in texture, or the overall, qualitative aspect of the piece. As with line, the multimodal meeting of movement and sound has implications for the weaving of texture. In each of these performances the sonic texture—the tissue of pitches, harmonics, strikes and other sounds coming from the double bass—moves both with and against the physical texture, which is to say the density, intensity, velocity and so forth of the dancer's movements.

With the addition of dance into the formal equation, sonic texture isn't just a matter of surface changes unfolding in time but instead becomes something comporting itself in a three-dimensional space. When counterpoint includes a dancer's projections and extensions in space, textural density becomes a blend of thickness of depth as well as density of surface. Similarly, textural saturation—the intensity of the overall sound—opens up to include the intensity of movement and of the dancer's confrontation with the surrounding space. Under these conditions texture is transformed from a quality of surface to a quality of mass.

Spatialization of Sound

Given the expansion of texture from surface to mass, the musical half of the duet becomes spatialized in an aesthetically significant way. Sound already possesses a spatial dimension—it always comes from a particular place. Varèse, in noticing this phenomenon, evocatively described it as a kind of sending forth. In a purely musical work this spatial dimension of sound tends to elude notice unless deliberate attention is called to it as when, for example, a score or performance calls for instruments to be positioned at distances from each other within the performance space. In the context of dance, with its focus on physical forms distributed in space, the spatial location of the sound naturally emerges as an aesthetic element in its own right—as a formal component of the overall performance. In tandem with awareness of the dancer's movements we become aware of the sound source as being here and not there, of the sound as projecting itself along a certain spatial path analogous to the dancer's path through the space.

This spatialization of sound can be exploited in ways that have a bearing on the contrapuntal relationship between dancer and musician. Consider Orrù's choice of playing from a stationary point at the top of the stairs that Spada dances down. His projection of sound from that steady point, combined with his choice of tones and articulations, gives his line a spatially stable, planar quality in relation to the moving body of the dancer, which we can imagine as a now curving, now angular object tracing a path in three dimensions across a plane. In my duet with Ken I made a similar decision to remain stationary—certainly not a difficult choice when one is playing an instrument with the size and bulk of a double bass—and to project sound along a linear vector as a ray would project from the center of a circle. In fact as our duet developed, this sonic vector defined the space as a section of a kind of imaginary sphere, with the endpin of the bass at the center, the sound projecting outward from it like a radius, and Ken's movements tracing arcs along the surface.

Gesture as Movement

The consideration of texture from a three dimensional point of view not only means that sound becomes something spatial as well as temporal, but that the visual element of the music—the sight of the physical gestures producing the sounds—will enter into the overall weave of the performance as well. Playing an instrument becomes, in its own way, a form of movement, a physical counterpoint to the dancer's movement. This will be true of any instrument, but the double bass is particularly exemplary in this regard. The instrument's size and scale require large gestures to produce a sound, even a subtle or quiet sound. (That the instrument itself has a human-sized physical presence would even seem to make it a quasi-independent participant in the performance.) The motions of Ken's arms, hands, head, legs and torso imitate, oppose, confront or evade the movements of my hands, arms, and bow as I finger, strike, pluck or draw the bow across the strings. Spada's movements set up a similarly complex relationship to Orrù's gestures, developing slowly and in increments while Orrù bows with alternating slow and rapid rhythms, accelerating as the bow rises and falls with greater sweep.

A Dialectic of Within & Without

As I hope the descriptions above demonstrate, the relationship between the two halves of these duets is a multi-faceted one. I want to suggest that its nature is mutually constitutive, that is, that each half shapes the other at a fundamental, formative level. But it does so in a paradoxical manner. This paradox consists in the ability of each half to absorb and assimilate the influence of the other without losing its own identity. Thus the performance of each participant molds and indeed creates that of the other in a sense, while each at the same time conserves the qualities peculiar to his or her own distinctive medium. Sound and movement interweave and yet at the same time each remains within its own modality, maintaining itself as a semi-independent aesthetic set of events defined by its own inherent qualities and yet whose shape is profoundly influenced—it wouldn't be too much to say "formed"—by the activity taking place in the other modality. The relationship between sound and movement in these duets, in other words, is both internal and external all at once; it is an ongoing dialectic of within and without.

Actions taking place internal to one modality—the crafting of a pitch sequence on the one hand, or the improvisation of a series of dance phrases on the other—will affect corresponding actions internal to the other modality. To this extent, the relationship is an internal one. From my personal experience, I know that the speed and angle at which a dancer manipulates an arm or pivots at the waist, for example, will have an effect on the factors internal to the shaping of the phrase I create contemporary to that movement, molding its tempo, the duration of individual pitches or rests, and its expressive dynamics. All of these musical variables—tempo, duration, dynamics—are present to me as possibilities, but it is the specific action of the dancer, drawn from his or her own set of possibilities, that triggers the choices that convert these possibilities into the sounds that are actualized in the way that they are in the concrete situation we share. When Ken's choices enter into my own sphere of awareness, the phrases, sounds, rests and so on that I play are in effect a way of making heard Ken's movements and stillnesses as they are for me at that moment, entering into and influencing the logic of my own line. Because the possibility of making a specific musical choice is internal to the development of the performance, any factor that affects that choice is related to the development of the performance internally.

And yet at the same time, the variables or parameters specific to one of the disciplines alone will have a bearing on each other independent of any influence coming from the other discipline. The musical phrase's pitches, dynamics, timbres, and rhythms are mutually affecting, providing it with an internal logic that projects it forward. Through a kind of dialectical turn, the mutual influence of purely musical parameters defines what is internal to the musical phrase and redefines the relationship to the dancer's actions as an external one. Relative to the purely internal relationships of musical parameters to each other, the dancer's movements are disclosed as necessarily external—they inhabit a different modality, defined by different parameters and a formal vocabulary of its own. The same can be said, *mutatis mutandis*, of the variables at play within the dancer's unfolding performance. They too define the relationship of the movement to the sound as necessarily an external one.

It's important to point out that this analysis is something that comes after the fact of participation. As engaged participants, our experience of the duet consists in a more immediate, implicit grasp of the situation. Our awareness of the internal relationship between our actions and those of our partner just is our awareness of our partner's actions as they impinge on our own; our awareness that the relationship to our partner is an external one just is the sense that, e.g., musical phrases "play themselves" according to their own internal logic.

Both/And

The relationship between sound and movement as separate expressive modalities may by definition be an external one, but as their interactions show, the boundary between them is permeable. The existential situation of the duet—its concrete reality—is of symbiosis even if its analysis is unavoidably expressed in the apparently conflicting language of interiority and exteriority. But any such conflict is just that—apparent. I want to suggest that to describe the relationship between movement and sound in these duets as external or internal is to name two aspects of a single phenomenon roughly analogous to describing the planet Venus as alternately "the morning star" or "the evening star." Both descriptions indicate the same object, but under different aspects given different frames of reference. So I would argue is the case with describing the relationship between disciplines in cross-disciplinary work as either external or internal. It is in fact a both/and proposition in which each component is out there in the other, is constituted as much by the other as by its own techniques, conventions and sensibilities.

One final metaphor. Imagine the interaction between dance and sound as taking place across a kind of tension field, with movement and sound pushing and pulling at each other, exchanging energies in precisely the complementary way that Baudelaire describes in the epigraph above.

NOTES

Free Improvisation & How It Means

Works Consulted:
Burkert, Walter: *Structure and History in Greek Mythology and Ritual* (Berkeley: U of California Press, 1982)

Writing Pushed Beyond Writing ·

Quotes from Jim Leftwich and Tim Gaze are from Jim Leftwich, *Asemic Writing: Definitions & Contexts: 1998-2016* (Roanoke, VA: TLPress, 2016).

Also referenced: Giorgio Agamben, *Language and Death: The Place of Negativity*, tr. Karen E. Pinkus with Michael Hardt (Minneapolis: U of Minnesota Press, 1991).

Is Silence Golden?

Works Cited:
André Breton, "The Automatic Message," in *What Is Surrealism? Selected Writings*, edited and introduced by Franklin Rosemont (NY: Pathfinder, 1978).

___, "Is Silence Golden?" in *What Is Surrealism? Selected Writings*, edited and introduced by Franklin Rosemont (NY: Pathfinder, 1978).

___, *Manifestoes of Surrealism*, tr. Richard Seaver and Helen R. Lane (Ann Arbor: U Michigan Press, 1972).

___, *Surrealism and Painting*, tr. Simon Watson Taylor (New York: Harper & Row/ Icon, 1972).

De Chirico, Giorgio, "*Point de musique*," in *L'Art métaphysique*, ed, Giovanni Lista (Paris: L'Echoppe, 1994).

Atopia: Soundings from Non-places

Works Consulted:
Marc Augé, *Non-places: An Introduction to Supermodernity*, tr. John Howe (London: Verso, 1995).

Franco Rella, "The Atopy of the Modern," in Giovanna Borradori, ed., *Recoding Metaphysics: The New Italian Philosophy* (Evanston, IL: Northwestern U Press, 1988).

Imaginary Numbers

Works Consulted:
André Breton, "Ascendant Sign," in *Free Rein*, tr. Michel Parmentier and Jacqueline D'Amboise (Lincoln, NE: U Nebraska Press, 1995).

Michel Carrouges, *André Breton and the Basic Concepts of Surrealism*, tr. Maura Prendergast (University, AL: U of Alabama Press, 1974)

Ferdinand Alquié, *The Philosophy of Surrealism*, tr. Bernard Waldrop (Ann Arbor, MI: U of Michigan Press, 1965).

The Silver Age of Surrealism in Exile

Works Consulted:
André Breton, *Arcanum 17*, tr. Zach Rogow (Los Angeles: Sun & Moon Press, 2000).

Works Cited:
Ferdinand Alquié, *Philosophie du surréalisme* (Paris: Flammarion, 1955).

André Breton, *Manifestoes of Surrealism*, tr. Richard Seaver and Helen R. Lane (Ann Arbor: U Michigan Press, 1972).

___, "Nonnational Boundaries of Surrealism," in *Free Rein*, tr. Michel Parmentier and Jacqueline D'Amboise (Lincoln, NE: U of Nebraska Press, 1995).

___, "On the Survival of Certain Myths and on Some Other Myths in Growth and Formation," in *What Is Surrealism?: Selected Writings*, edited and introduced by Franklin Rosemont (NY: Pathfinder, 1978).

___, *Surrealism and Painting*, tr. Simon Watson Taylor (New York: Harper & Row/ Icon, 1972).

Robert Hobbs, "Surrealism and Abstract Expressionism: From Psychic Automatism to Plastic Automatism," in Isabelle Dervaux, *Surrealism USA* (New York: National Academy Museum in conjunction with Hatje Cantz Publishers, 2005), pp. 56-65.

Robert Motherwell, "The Modern Painter's World," in *The Collected Writings of Robert Motherwell*, ed. Stephanie Terenzio (Oxford: Oxford U Press, 1992), pp. 27-35.

Gordon Onslow-Ford, "Notes sur Matta et le peinture, 1937-1941," in exhibition catalogue, Paris, Musée national d'art modern, 1985.

P.D. Ouspensky, *Tertium Organum* (New York: Alfred A. Knopf, 1930).

Wolfgang Paalen, *Form and Sense* (New York: Arcade Publishing, 2013).

W. Jackson Rushing, "Ritual and Myth: Native American Culture and Abstract Expressionism," in Maurice Tuchman, ed., *The Spiritual in Art: Abstract Painting, 1890-1985* (New York: Abbeville Press, 1986), pp. 273-295.

Martica Sawin, *Surrealism in Exile and the Beginning of the New York School* (Cambridge MA: MIT Press, 1997).

Sidney Simon, "Concerning the Beginnings of the New York School 1939-1943: An Interview with Robert Motherwell Conducted by Sidney Simon in New York in January, 1967," in David and Cecile Shapiro, eds., *Abstract Expressionism: A Critical Record* (Cambridge U Press, 1990).

Dickran Tashjian, *A Boatload of Madmen: Surrealism and the American Avant-Garde 1920-1950* (New York: Thames & Hudson, 1995

Seven Theses on "the Emotional Life of Words"

Work referenced:
André Breton, "Marvelous versus Mystery," in *Free Rein*, tr. Michel Parmentier and Jacqueline D'Amboise (Lincoln, NE: U of Nebraska Press, 1995).

As Within So Without

Works Consulted:
Luciano Chessa: *Luigi Russolo, Futurist: Noise, Visual Arts and the Occult* (Berkeley: U California Press, 2012).

Herschel B. Chipp, ed.: *Theories of Modern Art* (Berkeley: U California Press: 1968).

Ester Coen: *Boccioni* (New York: Metropolitan Museum of Art, 1988).

Francesco Grisi: *I Futuristi: I Manifesti, la poesia, le parola in libertà, i disegni e le fotographie di un movimento "rivoluzionario," che fu l'unica avanguardia italiana della cultura europea* (Roma: Gran Tascabili Economici, 1994).

F.T. Marinetti: *Teoria e invenzione futurista*, L. De Maria ed. (Milano: Mondadori, 1983).

The Anti-Metaphysical Metaphysician

Works Consulted:
Paolo Baldacci, tr. Jeffrey Jennings, *De Chirico: The Metaphysical Period 1888-1919* (Boston: Bulfinch Press, 1997).

Piero Bigongiari, presentazione, *L'opera complete di Carrà dal futurism alla metafisica e al realismo mitico 1910-1930* (Milano: Rizzoli Editore, 1970).

Guiliano Briganti e Ester Coen eds., *La Pittura metafisica* (Venizia: Neri Pozza Editore, 1979).
Massimo Carrà, ed.; Caroline Tisdall, translator, *Metaphysical Art* (New York: Praeger, 1971).

Paolo Fossati, *La "pittura metafisica"* (Torino: Einaudi, 1988).

Viktor Shklovsky, *Bowstring: On the Dissimilarity of the Similar*, Shushan Avagyan, translator (Champaign, IL: Dalkey Archive Press, 2011).

On Russell Atkins: The Poetics of Objectified Mind

Works Cited:
Russell Atkins: *Juxtapositions* (Self-published, 1991).

Gianni Vattimo: "Art, Feeling and Originality in Heidegger's Aesthetic," in *Art's Claim to Truth*, ed. Santiago Zabala, tr. Luca D'Isanto (NYC: Columbia U Press, 2008).

The Enigma of the Hour

*Establishing the correct dates for de Chirico's paintings is notoriously difficult. My source for dates is Paolo Baldacci, *De Chirico: The Metaphysical Period*, tr. Jeffrey Jennings (Boston: Bulfinch Press, 1997).

Quotations from de Chirico's manuscript texts are taken from the edition collated and dated by Giovanni Lista in *L'Art métaphysique*, ed. Giovanni Lista (Paris: L'Échoppe, 1994). Other editions and arrangements of the various texts exist. All translations are mine.

Sticks & Stones in the Time of Objects

All quotes are taken from the May 30, 2011 interview with the artist that appeared in CalRutgers4art, *"Guest Spot: Brian Olewnick.*

About the Author

Daniel Barbiero is a double bassist, composer and writer in the Washington DC area. He has been active in improvised and experimental music and dance in the Baltimore-Washington area as a performer, composer and ensemble leader since the early 2000s. His music is informed by his background in modal and free improvisation as well as the interpretation of indeterminate compositions; as a composer, he creates verbal, graphic and other scores using non-standard notation for soloists and small ensembles. He writes on the art, music and literature of the classic avant-gardes of the 20th century as well as on contemporary works for the online arts journal *Arteidolia* and has been a regular contributor to *Avant Music News*, *Perfect Sound Forever* and *Percorsi Musicali*, and served as an editor of the online arts journal *Bourgeon*.

danielbarbiero.wordpress.com

www.ingramcontent.com/pod-product-compliance
Lightning Source LLC
LaVergne TN
LVHW091149080826
845145LV00008B/2315